The Will of a Dying Artist

poetry & prose

Gale Thyme

The Will Of A Dying Artist

This book

is dedicated to

all of us survivors.

I wrote this for

you and I

because

we're

still

here.

The Will Of A Dying Artist

Cover Illustration by Ellé Om //
Zelaluyolilelu on www.fiverr.com

First Printing, 2018

Gale Thyme

Contact me at galethyme@gmail.com

ISBN-13: 978-1722792060

ISBN-10: 172279206X

BOOKS

The Will Of A Dying Artist

Hear ye, Hear Ye!

Stretching Out

When Cut, Our Blood Drips With
Nobility

Clepsydra

Falling From The Second Star To The
Right

How Girls Stretch Into Women

Cover Letter To The Queen

What Happened To The Lion's Mane?

Never Hide What Was Up To The
Paintbrush To Decide

Makeshifter

Wherever Leads The Arms Of Venus De
Milo

Flying Without Boots

The Will Of A Dying Artist

Thirst

The Very Dark Door of 1964 and After The Fact and Before

Stripes & Spots

Listen Children, Wise Words From The Kings Tongue!

Subtitles

Anthropocentric

Politricks

Realpolitik

Causeries & Clishmaclavers

Feral Semantics

The Wilde Effect

The Newton Effect

1¢ per True Word

An Affair With What Could Be

PREFACE

Dear reader,

I hope this collection will serve as a safe space for you.

I hope that by reading these pages, you can find within yourself the will to continue living just as I have upon writing each page.

Here is what each book in this collection entails:

Book I: Goblin Be Grand!
(how being human feels)

Image

Self-Love

Growing Up

Book II: Not Far From The Fairies
(how one copes)

Fantasy

Dreams

The Will Of A Dying Artist

Friendship

Romance

Love
(in every form)

Book VI: *Zeitgeist*
(how remembering feels)

Memories

For The Old Soul
Ode To My Mother

Ode To My Brother

Book VII: *Asphodels*
(stories untold)

Abstract Illustrations
(in word form)

This book is for you.

Allow each word to reach out and touch you.

The Will Of A Dying Artist

with love, Gale

The Will Of A Dying Artist

The Will of a Dying Artist

What cannot be found
teases you there.
The purpose of living,
the breadth of the hair.
Why does he breathe,
when he breathes out fear?
Why does she march in the rain without care?
Seas pelt her skin but the stars in her eyes,
reveal a soul that's willful and wise.
Why paste ears on children
to hear evil and speak it?
Eyes to see lies
and tongues to leak it.
Why do I say what few understand?
Write mazes with fingers that men reprimand.
Why do you read
with a curious speed
and eyes that eat the pages?
Or fingers that feel the words,
tracing each line like birds in cages.
What can be found
will leave you soon.

The Will Of A Dying Artist

You wait for them,
they inhabit the moon.

Goblin

Be

Grand!

(how being human feels)

The Will Of A Dying Artist

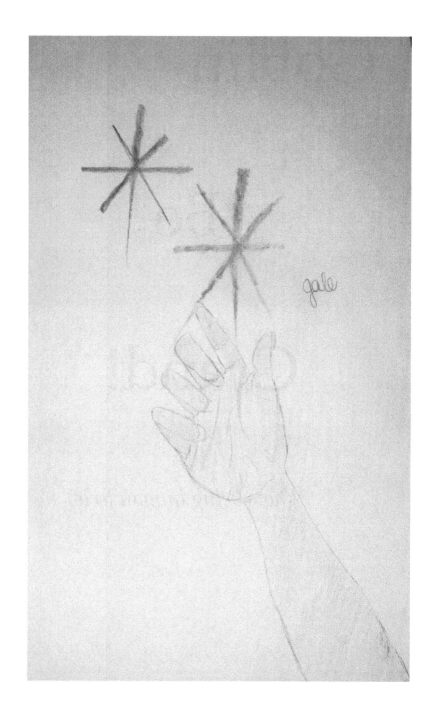

Goblin be **Grand!**

You have come from a land
where they've overfilled your lungs with the sea
and buried your detested body in the sweltering
sand.

You were abandoned.
They've left you on your own.
By the waves for many nights you were thrown.
Until your lifeless body found a foreign shore
and you risked opening your eyes though they
were sore
and you came across nothing more
than disbelieving eyes bounding your hands in ties
avoiding your desperate cries
and sharing amongst their tongues lies.

*"What of these warts on its stomach and bulging
knees?"*
*"It's purple tongue is throbbing as if it's been stung by
the bees!"*
To strike me down with coconuts, they climbed the
palm trees.

A mother scolded her son for approaching me
out of fear he'd catch fleas.

But he heeded her words not
and it was the ropes that he fought
and before I knew it, I was freed.

"I am as you are" claimed he.
*"Damned and distraught seem we. Without a pleasant
thought we be. Let us run from our troubles and sail the
great sea. And while we do we'll write poetry. We'll
deliver our book in the mind of a soul that feels poems
are a part of what makes them whole. "*

And so came a knock on my door
and before me was a basket filled with nothing
more
than a still, small heart dripping with blood
stuffed with poems written by hand
and as I rewrote them from my eyes flowed a flood.

Goblin be **Grand!**

The Will Of A Dying Artist

On The Edge Of 6

Floral wallpaper.
Wooden wardrobe.
Roses on dresses
and hats to match.
Onto mother I latch.
Cheetah print throw.
Baby is sleeping.
Feed her milk from your
breast.
Press her heart to your chest.
Give her love, let her rest.

Christmas in Florida.
Ribboned garland on door.
We roam the neighborhood
two times more.
Baby on bike
returns for a cheek kiss.
Reading from Peter Rabbit
all I felt was bliss.

The Will Of A Dying Artist

On The Edge Of 7

Quite curious how quickly
one's life can turn.
It was for a brother
I'd beg because it was
for a brother I'd yearn.
It was for a brother I'd yearn
because I hadn't a friend
on this Earth.
And soon before I knew
what was happening,
happening was
my brother's
birth.

A baby boy
with mother's face
and my eyes of brown.
I'd try to make him laugh
when his lips melted into a frown.

All happened so soon
and I wished to the moon
for a change.
It was my whole life
I wished to rearrange.
I sought adventure
but then again I suppose

The Will Of A Dying Artist

all children do.
I guess I was in constant
craving of something
exciting and new.
Nothing much has changed
since then, nothing much at all.
I'm still quite short, not very tall.
I haven't anyone to call.
I'm on the edge of 16
and I feel like fading away
even though there is so much
I haven't seen.
But I shan't
and I can't,
not yet at least.
There's much more
to be done before I'm released.
We, humans, must hang on
for at least another day before
we all fade away.
Hang on with me
and there shall be moments
upcoming
where we will have glee.

The Will Of A Dying Artist

On The Hum of A Lullaby Unsung

My baby, hush now.
The fields they plough.
And they silence the cats meow.
And they milk the cow.
And they gossip of us now.

I have brought you into this world, my child
but they shall convince you not to live.
Never mistake life for society.
And never forget if you have then you give.
And always migrate to where love fills the air
and pure laughter is near.
It's that bite-sized chest of yours that brews most
joy and care.
And one day you shall meet me where sky kisses
the Earth
And by then you will know your own worth.

But it's now we must part.
Your spirit is wise and your mind is art.
But don't follow me for I'm finishing before I can
start.
And this is for your sake and mine.
In this life, I haven't been fine.
God's allowing me to go.
So I just wanted to let you know
that you don't have to stand in the front of the line
and when they push you to the back, leave and
make your own.

The Will Of A Dying Artist

You belong to yourself, you are nobody's clone.
You were never a slave
so I expect you to behave
like the Queen/King I had you as.

The Will Of A Dying Artist

The Beggar

She was starving for the love that friendship could offer.

*Even if only a bite, she longed to
at least taste this fruit that everyone else was enjoying.*

*She had planned to suck out the juice and
savour the taste and enjoy the benefits to her health.*

*She wanted to give it a try if only to say that
she had eaten that fruit and recognized the taste.*

However, the fruit she was given was bitter.

*When she took a bite, she mistook water
for the juice everyone raved about.*

*And when she sank her eager teeth into the soft flesh of
the fruit,
she wondered why it didn't feel real on her tongue
or taste as good as she had witnessed others describe it.*

She only continued to bite into the skin of the fruit

The Will Of A Dying Artist

that would not allow her to peel it raw.

*Eventually, she decided to stop giving the fruit a try
altogether.*

*The people around her informed her that the juice
from the fruit was healthy for her brain, claiming that
eating
this fruit was absolutely necessary to add into her
lifestyle
and it was recommended to eat at least once a day to
keep the therapist away.*

*But as much as she tried,
her fruit refused to be peeled for her.
They were not her fruit to have and she was forcing them
open.*

*They came and went into her life, all promising to fill her
stomach
with nutrients and remain within her until time ended.*

*But into her stomach the worst of
fruits were swallowed down.*

The Will Of A Dying Artist

*And although all convinced her they would not leave her
body,*
twas only natural for her body to release toxic wastes.

And she could never release these wastes naturally.

*They had to be shot up through her throat
and purged out of her mouth.*

Unexpectedly.

The Will Of A Dying Artist

Peeling Potatoes

They sunk their eager teeth into my potato skin
and sucked all the vegetable oil from their meal
and doused the rest of me with gravy
and told everyone they knew that they loved
potatoes
because they had me.

But they never had me raw.
They had to cook me brown
and make me tasty
and personalize their custom made meal
so that I was to their individual likings.
I complied because I would've only been
ashamed to be a dry, hard and sour potato.

"You're not like other potatoes."
they claimed, spitfireing up faux flattery
as they ate me up until there was nothing left.
And it was then that I realized
the only reason I wasn't like other potatoes they
tried
was because other potatoes never let the human
beings
pick them from the garden
and perfect them to their liking
and eat them all up.

But by the time I had realized any of this
all had been done.

The Will Of A Dying Artist

I found myself in a mucky position,
much too tardy for what had been done to me.
I needed the time and care to grow again.

And that I did.
Only to be eaten up all over again
by more humans who didn't mind
eating potatoes raw.
How many times must I be reborn to stop myself
from trusting the humans?

The Will Of A Dying Artist

Farewell To Lucy

Swingsets and sunbeams
this is what it means
to play as a curious kid.

Over the mulch runs the fun loving friends.
Under the swing weeps the little girl blue.
Over the ropes hops the sweetest of gals.
Everyone's jumping but that excludes you.

"Give me a dollar and I'll be your friend."
says the baby that lives on the beach
to the loner without any father.
By the people around her, she's chained to a leach.
"Here comes she again, what a bother"

At recess, the children play tag
and of course she's never invited.
She lays in the grass and watches the clouds.
Into works of art they're united.

With a mind that's traveled to venus and mars
and a steady supply of books,

The Will Of A Dying Artist

she writes out adventures and stories of wonder.
Since playing alone attracts looks,
they're tongues are buzzing, with laughter they
thunder.

"Sandboxes with spirits are better than kinder"
she hopelessly mutters with a wail.
Only so much could them mocking her hinder
the beauty and time of her tale.

Prancing about with friends none could see,
a heart full of pain and a mind grown traumatic.
Spells from the tongue of a child seeking miracles,
the sad tale of the missing ecstatic.

Endlessly crying Virginia Woolf,
she's just as afraid as Martha.

Eating with ghosts can pass the time.
Today we shall play if you toss me that dime.

A figment of solitude, the result of a taunt.
A solemn reminder, a child to haunt.

The Will Of A Dying Artist

Farewell to Lucy, from you I've learned much.

The air I could feel but still never touch.

You extended a hand because nothing was there.

You were created so that when I cried someone

would hear.

The Will Of A Dying Artist

Afrodite

"How sweet!" remarked my nose
as I dozed off in a rose.

They could already fly, but my wings were built by
me alone.
"Why, those aren't *real* wings" mocked little Sara
Day.
"*My* wings are real but yours come off and can fly
away."
So my head hung low in shame
and I left them playing their game.
A game I couldn't play because we weren't the
same.

The following day, I arrived without wings
and was laughed at by two teeny tiny things.
"What happened to your *moth* wings? I thought
you could fly?"
"Her back is bare. She's not as pretty as I."
And they laughed and they laughed as I ran off to
cry.

I returned the next day with an apprehensive sigh.
I wore no wings upon my back.
And was reminded again of how much I lack.
The children played games and the pixies flew
high.
Male fairies ooed and awed at the pixies in the sky.
Sara Day had the wings of a butterfly.

The Will Of A Dying Artist

Kissing her lips was some self-absorbed guy.
She winked at me teasingly.

The next day I hadn't bothered to go to the school.
The teachers weren't fair, they thought me a fool.
Although I passed and worked by the rule.
I hadn't wings like they,
like little Sara Day,
who only passed because of compliments to the teacher she'd pay.

I climbed up a tree with a book instead.
For many hours I read and I read
until a small birdy climbed out of his bed
and looking at me scratched his little head.
"Hello and good evening. And who are you?"
asked the birdy who was tiny, plump and blue.
"I am a fairy without a wings."
"Without any wings? Why call yourself such things?"
chirped the bird while gathering a nest full of rings.
"I'm quite ugly. That's what I'm called by the pixies in class."
"The pixie in class? What a great ass! You should be in school now to learn and to pass."
The hoppity bird sorted his rings by size.
"No point to that for the teachers have bad eyes. From Sara Day they believe all the lies. Returning to school now wouldn't be wise."
"What does it matter if you can or can't fly? Sure, wings can be pretty just like whatever meets the

The Will Of A Dying Artist

eye. But what is the sense when we're all bound to
die? So you can't fly but you can walk and you can
read. There are things you can do that they can't.
And once you realize this then you shall be freed."
The bird then passed me one golden ring.
"I cannot fly like the rest but I sing. I earn my
money from doing my thing. Now make it through
school and read. When you look at my ring,
remember this deed. Remember all things great are
born of a seed. The day you'll feel greatness is the
day you are freed."

The bird hopped away that one Autumn noon.
He left on that day, left much too soon.
Over Sara they'd sigh and swoon.
I'd read my books and wish to the moon
not to fly but to be great and free
not to hate but to love and be me.
I found myself in poetry
and discovered that grace and art was beauty
and the only ugly was the act of the pixie that
heartlessly excluded me
and blinded my exquisite eyes with lies.
My will is a mountain and my mind is a sea.
I do not fly but I write poetry.
A fairy without wings, I am not she.
The poet that survived, shall always be me.
In order to grow, understanding is key.
And now that I do, I can be free.
Look at me fly, look at me!

The Will Of A Dying Artist

Grotesque

The large men
chased me down with
pitchforks and torches
and showed no mercy
as my grotesque face
pleaded for their sympathy
and demanded a reason for
such drastic, violent measures.
It was almost as if they were
deaf and seeing was all they could do,
their eyes served as their conscience
deciding for them all they should do.
And upon observing this, being the clever
creature I was, I used my better wit and
undressed myself completely.
And before them lay the body of a trembling
human woman sprawled
out on the forest floor,
chained to their carriage.
And so what more could their
compassionate,
masculine hearts do but aid a
damsel in distress?

The Will Of A Dying Artist

Flesh and Bones

Sugar for breakfast.
Pudgy is me.
That's all the human eye can see.
She's built of fat, he's made of muscle.
If you want to be loved then you must hustle.
Why doesn't she like the thighs with the meat?
The fat spreads out when she takes a seat.
Run, jump, run to get the treat.
These breasts are too big, they're hurting my back.
My bras are too thin, it's more space they lack.
I could never be a Victorian.
Corsets would undo themselves.
Circulation would be thin.
On Monday, I ate the milky way.
Today, I settled for Pluto.
My porcelain dolls have nothing to say
but they're as fat as I, you know.

The Will Of A Dying Artist

The Third Lost Girl
for every captain hook

I was born with the features
that men are repulsed by
and women mock.

Upon leaving my mother's
womb, I was never informed
that the creatures of the planet
I was entering would judge me
so as if I am expected to not have
come out the way I did.

I asked a pirate to help me
replace them so he lead me
aboard his flying ship and gave
me hooks where beauty used to
occupy.

Because the crocodiles were so
hungry, I gave them the human
limbs they sought for their supper.
With all the loveliness from my
body now a part of their stomachs,
I am certain they feel whole now.

The Will Of A Dying Artist

Ideally

Woman/Man be *flat*.

Woman/Man be *round*.

Woman/Man be *lost*.

Woman/Man be *found*.

Woman/Man listen to my

every word without

murmuring a *sound*.

Echo my every *move*.

Love me so love to

none I can *prove*.

The Will Of A Dying Artist

Hear Ye, Hear Ye!

If he/she doesn't jump at every opportunity to see you, then he/she doesn't want to.

If he/she doesn't hang onto your every word like he's/she's hanging onto dear life, then he's/she's not listening.

If he/she only compliments the features of your body as if there's nothing more, then that's the only part of you he/she loves.

If he/she never goes out of his/her way for you whether that be through a call or a letter, then he/she never thinks of you.

If he/she doesn't accept your faults even when he/she can't understand them, then he/she doesn't want you anymore.

If he's/she's never been there for you when you've needed him/her the most, then he/she doesn't care enough.

The Will Of A Dying Artist

If he/she asks you to change for him, he'll/she'll
never be satisfied with the clothes you've bought.

If you feel like he's/she's avoiding you, that's
because he/she *is.*

We only perceive incorrectly and misinterpret, but
what we feel is never wrong.

If he/she doesn't make you feel the love you
deserve to be receiving upon giving your own love
in return, then he/she doesn't love you.

It's okay to let go of the rose if the thorns are only
making you bleed.

Watch as each petal is lifted away by the air you
blow
and allow yourself to receive the love from
yourself that he/she failed to supply.

The Will Of A Dying Artist

Stretching Out

I'm beginning to see myself
in a whole new light.
I am not a length, a width nor
a height.
I'm transitioning, you see,
into the woman I hope to be.
Unshifted is my will and
motherly is my nature.
I must remain vigilant and still.
I must stand tall though short be
my stature.
My place is wherever my heart
wills it to be.
I am a mountain instead of a tree.

The Will Of A Dying Artist

When Cut, Our Blood Drips With Nobility

My mother is a woman, indeed.
Her legs sway wildly instead of remaining frozen
in a strut.
Her hips are a flexible current, an uncertain tide.
She speaks, now, with an accent from the island
an accent that the sea, herself, has longed to mimic
many times.
A tongue stolen from some English and some West
African
grounded into something quite beautiful and rough
that
can be soft and pretty when it pleases.
She explains to me the flags of the world
as if she painted them all herself.
My mother's face is beauty itself
when she smiles at children purely
and scrubs it after a long, hard day
wiping all of the makeup away for
the goddess to shine through.
And any man who can't see this
isn't worthy of her.
To win the heart of a lioness and a Queen

The Will Of A Dying Artist

is an honor one should never take for granted.

And, mother, I shall never allow myself to be won
over too easily.

For, I'd rather not be won at all.

Within your face, I see worth and love and beauty
and truth.

And I know all of these traits have been passed
onto me.

Therefore, I know how to rule my own kingdom
and I can see lies through the eyes of Kings
and I can know whether one is worthy for the
position
to merge our lands together
and rule with me.

The Will Of A Dying Artist

Clepsydra

I **hear** myself growing upwards
upon hearing myself speak
as if the world is coming to an
end instead of just beginning.

I **see** myself growing upwards
upon allowing the little girl of
my heart to remind this strange
woman the outspoken politics
of a child's will.

I **watch** myself growing upwards
at times I completely lose sight of
why it is children do what they do
when my mind is striving to achieve
fluency in the dialect of the adult.

I **smell** myself growing upwards when
the scent of the flowers I tend to daily
begin to seem unfamiliar since I've forgotten
to add savouring their aroma to my daily
routine.

I **feel** myself growing upwards
upon stretching myself out
instead of allowing myself to be
stretched every which way.

The Will Of A Dying Artist

I begin to **touch** this weird woman
and wonder why her body doesn't
feel like my own and wonder how
she moved into my body so fast.

I fancied myself much too stubborn for
my fixed mind to be taken over by anyone
that wasn't me.
But after observing this woman
I began to understand her a bit more
prompting me to realize that she was me
and she did belong to this body.
She was just yet one version of
my potential.
A stretched out,
adaptation of not what I'd desired
to be but what I had to die to become.
A living piece of proof of what
humans are capable of.

The Will Of A Dying Artist

Falling
From
The
Second
Star
To
The
Right

16 is near.
I'm almost there.
What's scary is I feel the same.

I've made it to this year
and though none but I care
if anything I've abandoned my tame.

Mommy rocked me in her homely arms at birth
and over the years I forgot my worth
though I seemed to have known it back then.
I've had to carry myself though I still don't know
how.
I'm not a good mother to me, I'm not my own frau.

I'm still but a girl
and I fear this world greatly.
And I've been acting quite immature lately.
I prefer children to adults because
they say what they feel
and the more elders I meet

The Will Of A Dying Artist

the less they seem real.
I fear what is fake
because I can't understand it.
They smile at you as you walk
but gossip because you didn't sit.

I thought that by now I'd be acting my age
instead of writing with rage
because I feel I'm locked in a cage.
But I can't criticize me
since it's for me I must care.
I scold my poor mind when
she deals with enough.
I don't know what's wrong
with her but I shouldn't be rough.
I hate her.
I love her.
She's got guts and she's tough.
But I wish she'd stop trying to kill me.
And here I am on the edge of 16.
For making it here I shall crown myself Queen.
My voice is unheard and my words are unseen.
But this does not matter because we are one in the
same.
My art is my glamour.
Chapter titles are my name.
My heart is a castle that will never tumble.
My tongue always mocks me,
it speaks low and does mumble.
But I must admit I have come a long way.

The Will Of A Dying Artist

Although I feel soft, I'm a mountain in the making
and not clay.

The Will Of A Dying Artist

How Girls Stretch Into Women

Are the words you speak your own?
When you banter on the phone
mimicking phrases overheard throughout your
day.
What makes you act the way you do?
How am I to know your words are true?
We spoke before but now you've gone away.

I'm spilling out my soul
but to you I am a foal
whinnying to amuse you from the fence.
You stuff my mouth with hay
because what I have to say
to you doesn't make any sense.

Why is it I speak
why is it magic that I leak
to travel through your ears and warm your heart.
But you're paying me no mind
because I'm not the bucking kind.
You place a bridle on my jaw before I start.

But you just don't understand
that I am not a steed.
You upon my back
is the last thing that I need.
You give me apples everyday
but it's myself that I can feed.
You want to show me the way

The Will Of A Dying Artist

when I was born to lead.
And if you don't believe me
it's the stars you need to read.

Maybe horse is in my nature
this is how I act
but my soul watches for danger
and this I know for a fact.
It won't be a roar you hear
since I am not afraid.
You're sitting on a lion's back
even though I've neighed.

Don't mistake the things I say
for what I'm bound to do.
It takes awhile for me to pounce
It's a pattern I must first view
but once it comes time to hunt
no matter how you woo
no amount of tape or glue
can mend an eardrum split in two
from the trauma of the lions roar
that does not mew
or coo
but exposes to light all that is true.

You act like a fool
yet treat *me* like the mule
because to you I am a tool.
You're using me the way you've used other screws

The Will Of A Dying Artist

and why your plan isn't working you haven't any
clues.
But I'll tell you why
and I shan't lie
I simply can't be used.
I have my own way for everything
and by yours I was never amused.

The words you speak are not your own
and I'd much rather gallop off alone
than to be ridden by a man with a whip
until my back is bruised.

The Will Of A Dying Artist

Cover Letter to the Queen

Maybe I cast on too slow
and my hands weaved a ribbon instead of a bow
and there are many stitches I still do not know.
But the needle pricked my scars and dug into my
skin.
Maybe the yarn was too thick or too thin.
Maybe the thread took too long to go in.
Maybe my colors are not art but a sin.
I tied knots through my flesh and pulled thread
through bone.
I allowed all within me to be revealed and sewn.
I've used no ruler, machine nor guide.
I haven't allowed thick fuzz or loose strings to hide.
I haven't had anyone sewing by my side.
I did not sketch with geometry.
I sat with my yarn and let the needles knit me.
I opened my eyes and before me was cloth.
Not the latest frill of the dress or the wing of the
moth.

The Will Of A Dying Artist

Or the rip in the jeans or the crop of the shirt.
Only a blood-stained handkerchief mixed with
leaves and dirt.
And words never said.
And hurt.

The Will Of A Dying Artist

What Happened To The Lion's Mane?

Why do you speak in riddle and rhyme
as if I'm too young to understand what you mean?
I dissect every word given each and every time
even if you thought that your metaphor was never
seen.

Whenever I speak it is from the heart
even when I'm weak before I can start.
I blabber too much and too much is revealed
but there's little I can contain or keep concealed.
I'm just too direct and honest and true.
I trust way too much but what else can I do?
I know that it's smarter and safer to be wary
and hopefully one day I will.
Hopefully I can say *no* a little more
and be flexible instead of standing still.
And maybe I say *no* too much
and humility is what I need as I'm told.
But I feel there's a lot I do censor
It takes awhile to ask for a blanket when I'm cold.
And I'm told to lean this way
and this person knows the right way
and the other has something better to say
and I should listen to both because they know more
than I.
But what if *I* feel that neither are true?
What is it then that I do?
I must humble myself and with this I agree

The Will Of A Dying Artist

because I do admire this quality
and I like to hear every story
but they do not make up my mind for me.
No one can tell me which way to be
because when it dwindles down to it
I can only be me.
And strive to be the best me I possibly can be.

And we must lift up our fellow man
and acknowledge that they're trying
because if they weren't trying, they'd only be
dying.
But I suppose they are living
because there's something they're giving.

And you, yes you, you're trying very hard.
In you there is worth, although by their words
you're scarred.
I know they called you worthless but does this
make you what you be?
And I know there is worth within you, for this I can
see.
Maybe I don't know you and you don't know me.
Maybe you don't fancy my style of poetry.
But at least it's your very best you are trying
and this I admire.
Maybe it's illness you're fighting and maybe you're
dying
but I'm glad you're still alive so that I could try to
lift you higher.

The Will Of A Dying Artist

And perhaps this didn't do the trick but at least my
intentions were right
and I did try.
And I know you do too.

So allow yourself to bow your head in despair
when the feeling is near
and when it isn't fill your mind with cheer.
And just let yourself be.
From their biased opinions it may be best to flee
because then you may feel a bit more free
and with freedom follows the ability to see.

The Lion hadn't a clue he was a lion at all.
The tigers told him to trim his mane because it
made his head appear too tall.
And eventually he longed for his full head of hair
but could not find this gift growing there.

The Will Of A Dying Artist

Never Hide
What Was Up To The Brush To Decide

Paint my body brown
and I shall never frown.
Such beauty
causes corners of mouths to drool
and eyes to dilate
like a fool
and God's to sigh
and clouds to cry
out of a fascination for art
that roams beyond the
fields of the mind,
inspires all
and warms the heart.

Paint my body the color of cream
so that my cheeks can glisten and gleam
a rosy red that causes minds to be fed
with flirtsy thoughts and words never dared
to be said.
From a moist pallette onto canvas
brushes sway to conceive
one with the skin of a pale Greek.
Don't be shy, go on and speak
about the beauty that exists
in the humans we are.

The Will Of A Dying Artist

Embrace your very own birth suit.
Come close to me, not far.

Paint my body the color of the sun
and from this gift I vow not to run.
How majestic would I appear
to glow here in the snow
and shine in the sun over there?
On each bristle colors are mixed
and tested and on you, your artist
used more than one brush.
From golden victorian clocks,
they stole velvet time; so when working
on you they wouldn't be in a rush.
Are those that mock you any more grand
than the artist who painted your image by
hand?
Heads only turn because you're a work of
art worth seeing.
You're a masterpiece
of a human being.

Paint my body the color
of the zebra's stripe
and for what would I have
to gripe?
Sun has placed a blessing
on the skin given to me
originally.
Bathe my skin in magical melanin
because I'd like to walk in the skin

The Will Of A Dying Artist

painted onto the man who came first.
Perhaps they shall treat me like the
worse
but I sense my days are too numbered
to bicker like an old bag about what my fellow
man had to say.
My shimmering lips smile
because I'm a great big pile
of art, humanity
and beauty.

Some are kissed by the sun
and others by the moon
and others by both
but to all, voices croon
because mankind is imperfect
in many ways
but our bodies are art
that we should maintain
and keep healthy
and custom to our souls liking
for all of our days.

The Will Of A Dying Artist

Makeshifter

This
soft here but rough there,
smooth here but full of hair
thick all over
bronze aged skin,
round as a rose toes,
stubby, runny nose,
breasts too thick for back,
waist sheltered by clothes,
down my legs lies a crack
dividing a flailing siren's tail into two
of a body
is but a makeshift
for this not long enough life
I'm stuck in.

Cleanse it everyday
though I may
this mind remains full of filth and abstracts and
everything in between
and this conscience remains full of guilt and doubt
and all things unseen
and my body is stout and not lean
and my mind only understands dates and times
but cannot find the object's mean

The Will Of A Dying Artist

and so what next after this life?
Perhaps another filled with more inspiration and
strife.
I doubt I'll ever miss what's happening now
and I'll be farther from what's been done before
right now.
This must be the last, now is the day.
All of my past is shoved away.
All that I do is my final chance.
I shall no longer run or dance.
I can only write and record
all that remains of my lives,
what I've learned,
and who all has
lead me to
eventually
become.

The Will Of A Dying Artist

Wherever Leads The Arms Of Venus de Milo

Because she was reaching for jollity,
her daring arms were sliced from her stiff body.
Why couldn't the rest of her move to express
how she felt?
To shake since she was trembling?
Her arms were the only parts
of her that could move and live
as if she were real.

Her arms gave her hope, deceiving her
into believing that perhaps, one day,
with nothing but these two arms and hands
she could be free.

But she perplexed the likes of others.
For they all desired the beauty they saw
in arms so hopeful, for their own.
She refused to ease the woes of the selfish,
desperate and distraught beggars who only
wanted to be caressed and instead continued
to use her arms in her own quest for freedom.
Upon seeing that freedom was never attainable,
her arms were taken from her
without her consent and
used up until they no longer

The Will Of A Dying Artist

possessed the will to move.

Her arms are no longer available at my disposal.
I haven't any hands to point and instill direction
within me, to show me the way to go and
demonstrate the decisions to make or all that
is right and just and fair.
I have only my own two hands, leading me to
where
I wish to be.

Dare I ever seek freedom, should I be humbled?
Should my own arms be sliced from my body
and given to others when my own hands had
never been anywhere and my own fingertips
have never touched anything to begin with?

The Will Of A Dying Artist

Flying Without Boots

These boots were made for walking.

So why do they remain still?

Anxiously rocking back and forth, instead of

marching up the hill.

This voice was made for moving,

the hearts of hardened men.

So why are magic thoughts whispered, and poems

written with pen?

Never to wander off the page, never to be seen

again.

This heart was made for loving, spreading love in

every way.

I'll love you again tomorrow, you only love me

today.

These hands were made for writing,

spilling pain into the ink.

Writing to live, writing so that every moment I

blink,

The Will Of A Dying Artist

will have purpose.

Writing is all I do.

Transcribing my soul unto paper and

sharing these words with you.

If I was made to write,

then why do I fear the bite

of the foreign eye judging as they might?

I write because I live.

There's something I simply must give.

These boots are motionless now,

but these hands are forming magic from dust.

And so this is why I must...

continue living.

Not Far

From

The

Fairies

(how coping feels)

The Will Of A Dying Artist

The Will Of A Dying Artist

Elves Dwell Within The Moon

Elves dwell within the moon.
"What sayeth thou?"
"She spoke too soon."

Pixies prance atop the hill.
"How dare she speak so?"
"I'm writing my will."

Gnomes preserve the treasure at night.
They shine the ruby's red with delight.
Spotted them I did, and oh what I sight!
"She's gone too far now."
"She must be mad."
"How nosy of she. To be nosy is to be bad."

But tis true! Tis true!
Good fay, please don't mind.
I am of the earnest kind.
I only wish to tell your tale.
Of me, you wrongly quale.
Now I shall speak of what it means
to live and love as a fairy does.
Disclosing all the obvious outliers of what is, what
will be and what was.

The Will Of A Dying Artist

A Day In The Life Of A Pixie

Last autumn, dead leaves fell all over the roof.

Sister likes dancing and brother's aloof.

Mother hates humans but I love them, you see.

It's because she's old-fashioned, a bad way to be.

Last Winter, we all saw a ravishing play.

I wish I could act but then mother would say

"Focus on sewing and surveying the soil.

For Earth to be happy we must work and toil.

Earth is a woman like you and me.

No matter the season, she likes to feel pretty."

To humans, I'm little.

I talk in riddle.

I'm cheeky and cherry and fun.

To birds, I am lazy.

I always sound crazy.

I'm too tall and I weigh a ton.

The Will Of A Dying Artist

Moss and Mudpies

By day, I live as a human but by night I love as a

fairy.

By day, I climb the trees but by night the palms and

I have the most thrilling of conversations.

By day, I fear the heights above me and fall on my

face and rub my sore feet but by night my wings

carry me off into times that have already been.

By day, I fill my body with sewer garbage and the

guts of things that once lived but by night I

consume sweet faerie wine from the King's golden

goblet and chomp down on the lettuce from

fairytale trees.

The Will Of A Dying Artist

By day, I only read of romance in books and stray

from the men who pass me by but by night I kiss

slimy toads into princes and jive in the slippers

other women cut off their toes to fit into.

By day, I lay in a dark room alone typing poetry

with all I have left and dreaming of far away lands

but by night I drift off asleep on moist lilies whilst

listening to the sound of the rain beat against the

leaves.

The Will Of A Dying Artist

The Curious Mortals Guide
To Interacting With Spirits

In order to see the fairies,
one must open both eyes
and *look*.

In order to hear the fairies,
one must block out each and every
distracting sound and remove the
wax from their ears and *listen* with
patience.

In order to gain the trust of the fairies,
one must *open* one's mouth
only when absolutely necessary
and allow polite honesty to drip
from their tongue.

In order to visit the land of the fairies,
one must allow themself to *rest* and
their mind to be clear and wander.
Fairies cannot occupy space that's
already full of matter.

In order to fly with the fairies,
one must first realize and *accept*
that they cannot fly on their own
because most mortals are not born
with wings.
Then they must choose a fairy worthy

The Will Of A Dying Artist

enough of their trust, tug onto their pant leg
and soar.

The Will Of A Dying Artist

Lore of the Lonely

Little Billie Seed
yearned to read
But couldn't because she was blind.

Flowers she wore
in her hair.
Fairies she swore
roamed near.
And if you weren't careful they'd prank you and
pull out your hair from behind.

She hadn't a friend at all.
Her hair stood up and she wasn't very tall.
So to blind little Billie I went
and informed her by none was I sent.
And over my face she felt and smiled.

"The fairies roam near" claimed Billie.
"A pixie watches you from that lily"
Though I fancied her mad, dared I nothing to say.
Her vision was bad but in trees she lay.
And to myself I thought, *"What a strange little
child."*

"I can see nothing but fairies"
said Billie with a handful of berries.
*"They guide me throughout my day…
…and in dreams we prance and play"*
and that was the last of Billie I saw.

The Will Of A Dying Artist

She went missing shortly after.
But whenever I passed the fields where we met, I
smelled berries and could hear her laughter.
Butterflies lead me to trees with faces.
I discovered mini mountains when I tripped on
shoe laces.
The fairies she saw I could feel,
I understood then they were real.
And that Billie Seed was never odd but just as a
fairy was, raw.

The Will Of A Dying Artist

Why
Dreamers
Live
In
Dreams

"Life imitates art far more than art imitates life." — Oscar Wilde, 1891 (The Decay Of Lying - An Observation)

Fantasy is not fiction
in my mind.
Perhaps
I can't
face
reality
but this
does not
mean I am blind.
If it fits into the puzzle
of life, love shall come my
way but for now I can indulge
in the pleasure of imagining bliss
instead of living out an imitation of this.
I struggle to see what there actually is to miss.

The Will Of A Dying Artist

Mrs. Silver-brimmed-round-top-hobby-clock's Shop

The clanging bell was sounded upon entering Mrs. Silver-brimmed-round-top-hobby-clock's shop that day with hopes of purchasing an antique pocket watch.
But everything in Mrs. Silver-brimmed-round-top-hobby-clock's shop that day wasn't available.
When I asked Mrs. Silver-brimmed-round-top-hobby-clock that day why none of her watches were available for purchase
Mrs. Silver-brimmed-round-top-hobby-clock turned to me anxiously and that day said to me "Because we're all out of time."
And so I left Mrs. Silver-brimmed-round-top-hobby-clock's shop that day, asking a passing gentlemen with a watch for the time.
And as we both stood outside of Mrs. Silver-brimmed-round-top-hobby-clock's shop that day he turned to me anxiously and said to me, "My watch doesn't work because we're all out of time."
And by the time I had glanced at his watch standing outside of Mrs. Silver-brimmed-round-top-hobby-clock's shop that day to proof-check the accuracy of his claim, I was out of time and he had departed from my side.

The Will Of A Dying Artist

And so I stood outside of Mrs.
Silver-brimmed-round-top-hobby-clock's shop that day and looked around me at all the people running this way and that with computers in their hands and distractions in their ears.
And I realized from observing the world around me standing outside of Mrs.
Silver-brimmed-round-top-hobby-clock's shop the truth in the words just recently spoken to me.
The world spinning around me was constantly losing itself to time it never had to begin with.
This peculiar concept was worshipped like a God and mentioned in the average man's mouth at least once per sentence.
And so I thought standing outside of Mrs.
Silver-brimmed-round-top-hobby-clock's shop that day "Do I live with love in my heart or time on my mind?"

The Will Of A Dying Artist

The First Lost Boy
to Peter Pan

"Oh sweet, dear child. Where to do you roam?" asked
the nosy, elder garden gnome.

"Uncertain am I. Somewhere very far from home."
responded the boy.
Through his bushy, knotted hair he ran a comb.

"Why is it far from home you seek?" continued the
gnome.
The boy, then, turned to face the gnome who at his
sack was taking a peek.

*"It's in man's nature to trek and venture. Sitting
around in nothingness, performing pointless, tireless
chores all my days is making me weak."*

"Ah, I see" And from the boy's sack, the gnome
snatched a fruit. *"May I, my boy? I do need the loot."*

The boy nodded and in turn the gnome thanked
him, gratefully.
But the boy turned his back and continued walking
hatefully.

*"Hey, there, don't leave! Before you do go there is plenty
of knowledge you have yet to know. If you don't know*

The Will Of A Dying Artist

where you're going, you'll go the wrong way. Come back
now, chat with me awhile, do stay. Learn all you can
about where you wish to be. That way, there'll be so
much more for you to see."

But the boy neglected to listen.
He did not study the map.
He trusted loosely because he knew not where he
was headed.
He walked and he walked until he walked into a
trap.

Fortunately for him, he found a way to break free.
He stole a boat and rode across the sea.
He fell asleep one night in the midst of a storm.
And awoke to find himself in a place that was
sunny and warm.

The Will Of A Dying Artist

The Fourth Lost Girl
for wendy; about the author

As a young girl,
an older girl
that attended my
baptism told me
that when I got
to be her age
I would stop believing
that fairies exist.
Upon asking her *why*
that is, she told me
that I would see when
I got to be her age.
Now, I'm around her age
and I've learned to see
more than the fairies
but the whole world around
me as a living, spinning
imitation of art.
Am I doing something wrong?
All is as it is.
We view the same portrait.
I suppose our eyes work differently.
Perhaps, I see too much
and she unconsciously
squints.

The Will Of A Dying Artist

Laughodil

She wore daffodil dresses

and dined with beetles at tree root picnic tables.

Chunks of peridots hung from her pointed ears.

Tall men never intimidated her

for she undid their ties and knotted up their hair.

She would often cameflague her laughing face onto

the bark of oaks.

Not a night went by when her pointed feet weren't

swelling with sores from swaying to the records

played by the soldiers at the camp.

Not a day went by when she wasn't flirting with

me or buzzing around lakes to greet turtles.

The Will Of A Dying Artist

Not a day went by that I couldn't recall her

laughing.

To me, she was joy itself.

She was a honeyed leaf that appeared normal at

first glance but always smelled sugary with a taste

that resembled syrup.

She left me by pecking my rosy red cheek with a

kiss, her long wild hair being blown behind her as a

breeze lifted her off into the heavens on a leaf.

Her life may have been short, but she chose to

spend it by making me smile

and teaching me to fly

and dancing

and doing as she pleased

The Will Of A Dying Artist

and always, always

laughing.

The Will Of A Dying Artist

Rhyme Heals All

Gayla Rhyme, Gayla Rhyme!
Slide me a name and I'll toss ye a dime.
I do need a nom de plume
so that of me they shan't wrongly assume.
Quick, please, Quick!
I'm running out of thyme.
But thyme does heal all.
Seasons the dish.
They say "Delish!"
Clears the nostrils of
crime
and
grime
just as
poor ideas
disintegrate
with
rhyme.

Malaise

(how dying feels)

The Will Of A Dying Artist

Pixie Soldiers For The Suicidal

Wisp,
O speck of light.
Float through the air.
Flicker and flight.
Latch onto my every breath with
all your might.
Renew my strength, enlarge my sight.
Extract from me
the urge to die
and dryeth each tear from my lid
as I cry.
Remind me of purpose when restraining breath
from my own lungs
I do try.
Stuff my mind with a will
to live.
Transport into my heart all your love
to give.

They fly to you from afar
and reach you wherever you are.
Sometimes they're the voice of a man.
Sometimes they whisper into your brain *"You can."*
They acknowledge the war raging on in your mind.
To the conditions of your brain they are not blind.
They'll play you a song, they'll show you a sign.
They'll let you feel as if you're fine.
They're not large enough to hug you
and most fairies are funny about being seen.

The Will Of A Dying Artist

They're tiny, trained soldiers.
They're caring and clean.
They'll remind you of purpose
and force you to hang on.
And when you fall they shall catch you
and show you your own individuality
reminding you that you are no man's pawn.

The Will Of A Dying Artist

How Feathers Fall

With words left unsaid, it ends.
One tear that continues to burn the eye but refuses
to escape.
She had felt more shame than love that day.
Floating from body to body —
each mind hooked to the time passer occupying
their palm.

Would she still lack purpose?
Without free will.
If she was born a beetle of the amazon or a cloud in
the sky.

By others who were told the same.
So that she may be told what to do and who to be.
She is taught language.

Then given every reason not to want it anymore.
Given life.
A child born anew.
The end has not yet arrived.
Time still remains.

Now read this poem from the bottom up.

The Will Of A Dying Artist

The Runaway Slave &
Her Forbidden Lover

Carry me current.
Shut my eyes with your salt.
Rock my body to sleep with your waves.
God's voice is hidden within the whispers of the
sea.

Carry me current.
I wish to be taken.
If these hands must take anymore,
they shall be bunched into a fist and cease to
function.
If these arms must carry any longer, they shall fall
from my shoulders.
This soul wishes to be held.

Carry me current.
I wish to speak man's tongue no longer.
Fill my lungs to the brim with the hymn of the
ocean.
I no longer wish to run

The Will Of A Dying Artist

I ran from everything
and was lead to you.

Carry me current.
I felt most free when the wind styled my hair.
You are controlled by air's breath and I am
controlled by you.
Land has trapped me.
The creatures that roam here have placed me in a
tiny box at birth.
They have labeled me all I'm expected to be and all
I'll ever be.
They have robbed me of money I do not have.
Children grow into machines that look down and
judge.
Land has locked me in a cage and chained me to its
roots.
Free me as the waves have no master.
Rust the metal of the chains I am locked in until it
snaps.

Carry me current.
My heart may stop as your own heart drowns me.
Fancy me mad as you wish for such a request

The Will Of A Dying Artist

but has my heart really ever beat as a slave to the
soil?
These brief moments of freedom are worth much
more
than the ability to run across fields only to return to
the cage.

Carry me current.
My dead body afloat in the water may be looked
upon with
sympathy by the creatures I once lived alongside.
But little do they know that the only thing that
sets me apart from them is the fact that
I am no longer a slave to man but a part of the sea.
You did not kill me.
It was the overfilling of love you clogged
my lungs with that left me breathless.

The Will Of A Dying Artist

Abroached

I raised the glass.
I tipped the wine.
I let it be known that all was fine.
Then all toppled over.
The cup was dense
and suddenly I could make sense
of what brought me to jump the fence.

The fence was set high.
Each wire impaled a cloud in the sky.
I fell upon my arse
dreading the day
I was forced to stay
and fancying my existence
a farce.

The Will Of A Dying Artist

Area 51

Everything beyond this point is confidential.
What is it you wish to see?
Though try as I may to conceal it all
it seems too trusting I always shall be.

I require more titanium from you.
With my reasons I'll remain obscure.
There's something I'm in the process of building.
There's certainty I need to ensure.

You brag of all your inventions
but I fear you intend to use them on me.
Instead of waiting for this time to arrive
and instead of planning out a plea
I'm working on my own so that I can be
protected from you
and all you may do.

This is my classified base.
This is my indifferent face.
I wish to keep locked my lips
and above the clouds my ships
and from you I'll struggle to conceal all
whatever the case.

The Will Of A Dying Artist

Mummification

Peel away my skin.
Strip me of my garments.
Remove the veil from around my head.
You shall find
beneath it all
a laughing
tirelessly
weeping
tirelessly
puzzled
child
dying for
something more.

Remove each and every bone.
If you search deep enough
you shall come across
not a soul
not a mind
but a heart.
Does it beat?
Does it bleed?
It tells you to be gentle.
That it longs for peace
from the panic
and assurety
from the
doubt
and

The Will Of A Dying Artist

solace from the life.

The Will Of A Dying Artist

Strings & Things

What am I
but an escapist
wasting away
the life
I was given by
waiting to die
and living for the
night I let my final
breath escape my lungs
whilst regretting
wasting away the life
I was given?

Yank the string
that is inevitably thin
through the hole of the
needle that is vaguely wide.
This is how we sew.
Is this how we live though?

The Will Of A Dying Artist

The Dancing Dust Pixie

Dust does not simply exist
but lives.
A speck of dust flew by and
landed on my victrola to dance
to all the 1930s tunes I've been
lying around weeping to.
See,
even dust pixies know how to
feel jouissance.

The Will Of A Dying Artist

Palliate
June 30, 2018

I'm beginning
to believe that
nothing has the
capabilities of
curing me.

To be put in
most simplistic
terms, there
is no cure for
what is not
understood.

The Will Of A Dying Artist

Vacuous
- *empty*

Even when every inch of me was pleading to die
and on the carpet I would lie
and my youthful body was shaking
because my corrupted mind was breaking
and my vision had abandoned both eyes
because my confused yet convincing mind
had threatened my weak heart into believe its lies
and something within my head was spinning
because at every attempt I was losing instead of
winning...

God forced my body to throw up all the
failed attempts at leaving that had been consumed
in the midst of giving into a mind I shall
always fail to understand
and forced my life to be resumed
and took me by the hand
and told me why I must continue to breathe
and told me that it's not my time to leave…

The Will Of A Dying Artist

Seeking Equanimity

I called the suicide hotline
because I was much too afraid to call you.
I sat in the cold, trembling with angst
scared of what my emotions would
bring me to do.

I know not what ails me
is it something in the air?
For everything, I'm demotivated.

I'd like not to be here.
I'd like to not be there.
I'd like not to be anywhere.
I'd like not to exist.

I no longer escape out of bed in the mornings.
At least I no longer slit my wrist.
I didn't know how to stop my mind
from trying to end my life so I wrote this
poem instead.
I don't think I can ever learn to live
with this head
for I'd rather be dead.

My mind needs a nice shower
and fresh seeds for gardens to grow.
My mind needs a break from the snow.
It's too cold up in there and my body's
beginning to freeze.

The Will Of A Dying Artist

I always feel weak in the knees.
I stutter when asking for help.
I no longer wish to yelp.
I wish all of this would end.
I wish I could call on a friend.
But grief to none I wish to send.

So I wrote this poem instead
because if I didn't let out the words
dying to be said
then my mind would've caused
me to be dead.

The Will Of A Dying Artist

Flurry

Last night rain drizzled
and this morning all was
pouring down.
Instead of seeking shelter
from the storm dripping from
my eyes, I allowed myself to
become drenched because
I'd decided, then, that I'd prefer
to have my entire body
soaked than to wander
into just any home uncertain of
its inhabitants and all taking place
behind closed doors.
The storm eventually calmed down
and now I'm drying myself off though
I know it'll always be drizzling and I'll
always be damp and never completely dry.
Should I reach out to a nearby shelter now
that the weather is calmer and I can see
better than before without the fog?
Or should I wait until I let go of all
and allow myself to lay in the rain
letting each and every drop
consume my quivering
body?
They say there's a cure
but I'm not so sure
if I believe them.
Everyone is seeking

The Will Of A Dying Artist

happiness.
It's the discontent,
like I, that find
themselves
dying
in the process
of emptying
themselves
out with
each
breath.

The Will Of A Dying Artist

Broach

Saying the words
"I tried to kill myself"
to another
living
breathing
soul
capable of thinking
you mad and
spreading your
personal trauma
to ears that don't
need to hear is almost
as frightening as allowing
the words
"I love you"
to fly from one's tongue
carrying this custom message
into the ears of another
living
breathing
soul
capable of thinking
you odd and
spreading your
personal emotions
to ears that don't
need to hear.

One person

The Will Of A Dying Artist

could be harnessing
both statements within
their hearts but are much
too afraid to say either.
Both statements require
us to strip ourselves away,
opening up our wounds
and giving others the
permission to rub salt
into them.

Perhaps these aren't
the wisest of words
to reveal to another
but they're certainly
some of the boldest.

One is a cry for help
because one heart could
no longer withstand the
torment and overflowing
of emotion it was being put
through.
The other is a cry for love
because one heart could no
longer withstand the torment
and overflowing of emotion it
was being put through.

It was your heart that brought
you to say such things, not you.

The Will Of A Dying Artist

Even when you are hurt as a
result of revealing either, you
must know that you *can* be happy
and in some moment in the future
either far or near you *will* feel happy
if you give yourself the permission to.
Don't block yourself from feeling when
you do feel.
Holding in your tears are not healthy.
Allow yourself to cry it all away.
Allow yourself to wipe it all away.
And allow yourself to feel more than just
fear.

Orwellian

Upon playing a video game
a thought occurred to me
that caused me to ask myself
what is the sense of collecting
all of these coins for myself
when one of the obstacles up
ahead is liable to kill me anyways?
It was then that I died and restarted
the game to try and get farther than
I had the last time I played.
However, this time I didn't pay as
much care to collecting coins
as I did the last time. I played simply
because I was told in the manual
that collecting coins was the object
of the game and the amount of coins
collected determined how well of a
player one was and had decided to devote
more care into running along.
If the game was not programmed to
keep me on my feet constantly,
trying to collect as many coins as I
possibly could, then perhaps there'd be
more time left to enjoy the run when I did
happen to run.
If only the game could've slow down for
me a bit more and included more than
one player then perhaps I wouldn't be
so tempted to stop playing.

The Will Of A Dying Artist

Ennui

I'd like to stop walking now.
Surely, you must apprehend.
The soles of my feet are aching with cramps.
I wear worn out shoes that none can mend.
I no longer bare a desire for lamps
when in dark rooms throughout the day
I lay.
I wish I was rapidly approaching the end
because within me lies little will to stay.
I wish I could move on and forget what has been
as quickly and simply as they have done.
Holding onto false hope feels like a sin.
I wish that from all I could run.
Tired I am,
truly you see.
No jogging
nor
skipping
nor
hopping
for me.
Neath sheets I lay
all day
just as on bloody sheets
I was born.
From mother's body
a cord was torn.
These clothes before
I have worn.

The Will Of A Dying Artist

Upon leaving this world,
I shall be gay.
There will be nothing
I'll be forced to say.
None shall threaten
to take my life away
when it is gone.
All shall judge me
for something I've done
wrong.
And all shall forget
whilst continuing along
with the life they love
and they hate.
One moment all
is fine and the next
all it great.
And then life is a louse
and the reasons they
struggle to find is why
on Earth they are being
treated so unkind.
Whether they love or hate
living they can hardly make
up their mind.
And then there are those like me
where whatever their life may be
their mind is set on leaving.
I suppose it's just
as they say:
the lack of sunlight I've been receiving.

The Will Of A Dying Artist

Unvermeidlich

Wenn ich schreibe nicht,
dann ich tot bin.

The Will Of A Dying Artist

The Feverish Ogre's Final Testament

What thinkst you?
Be there a cure for me
or must I go on feeling this way
for all of time?

Dare you come near me with that stick!
You'll hide it in my path and from behind me you
shall kick.
And fall, fall I know I will.
But nevertheless, this notion is absurd.
So I must keep locked my dolly lips
and remain still.

A raindrop pelted my tender skin yesterday.
I rubbed it off and ordered it to begone. To dry
away.
But it mocked me and called its friends and more
came along.
I could be seen there, an evershaking head attached
to a body in full tremble.
"It's just a little rain" claims Mother.
So why, then, am I acting out in a way that is
wrong?

I felt that the rain would seep through my skin and
wash all the blood from my thin veins.
I felt that the rain would give me a cold so that I'd
be forced to sit at home sick while Sally and Sam
went out to play.

The Will Of A Dying Artist

An ant approached me the other day and I flinched
back, frozen and alarmed
that my toes were about to be bitten and the heels
of my feet would burn and sting and I would be
severely harmed.
I suppose I was just afraid of possibility, what this
unpredictable thing might do.
Sam once informed Sally and I that a mite ate into
his shoe.
It's very possible that this eventuality could float
my way too.

I called for Sally a few weeks back but she never
checked in with me.
I called for her once more a couple days ago and
she acted like my call she did not see.
But, truth be told, she fancies me a ham
and enjoys time indulged in childish games with
Sam.
And I'm left abandoned as always I suppose.
The pain is confusing which is why I write it into
prose.

This morning, before it was here that I came
I called her and Sam again but received a response
of the same.
So I called for my mother, my sister and my brother
but they were all out with their own friends.
So I called on another.
Reaching out to those I haven't seen in awhile

The Will Of A Dying Artist

since they treated me the same as Sally and Sam
and I puckered up to kiss them pink and put on a
smile.
But it's me they have all chosen to avoid just as
before.
It's me they wish to mock and ignore.
To me, alone, they've all locked a door.
Oh, I feel much too much, doc.
When I'm pricked, I bleed.
I've kept this all hidden away before
but it's now I must concede.

What do ye think?
What do ye think?
It's this I die to know.
I lock myself away for the day.
It's nowhere that I go.
But why selfishly subject others to this guilt, this
shame, this woe?

*It seems to me you're planning your suicide. We need to
lock you away.*

Lock me away?
Lock me away?
No, no but what did I say?
I'd just like to know what is wrong with me and
how to get better.
I shall try.

The Will Of A Dying Artist

I felt upon leaving the session that I was being
judged for the weep and the cry.
I felt that I had exposed what shouldn't have been.
That there was no cure and giving myself away
was a sin.
And that maybe it's better to leave it growing
within.
The feelings, I mean.
A woman I am.
I'm emotion, I'm emotion
and not that of a Sam.
Limited are the use of my eyes.
I do not see but smell the pies.
I do not taste but savour
each and every flavour.
And this includes the bad.
Poison was what I had.
To my surprise, I still live.
I guess there is more I have to give
before my petals wilt and my dried out
anatomy is picked and thrown and stepped 'pon.
And I will never really be known.
But at least I gave it all a try.

What if all that I feel and think is a waste?
There'd be no need to display such haste.
To them I'm a turkey that they must baste.
They eat me and soon forget about the taste.

The Will Of A Dying Artist

Waiting To Live
the caterpillar's chronicles

I can't help but feel
like I'm wasting my youth.
Nothing seems real
and this is the truth.

Endlessly, I sing the blues.
At every game I tend to lose.
To perform everyday activities
I've begun to refuse.

I hardly leave home.
There's nowhere to roam.

I'm always alone.
None call on the phone.

I feel like I'm losing my mind.
The world seems too cold and unkind
to step foot onto the soil.
I suppose I must wait for the water to boil
before making tea.
However, I haven't any tea bags
so only hot water will there be
for me.

The Will Of A Dying Artist

The Second Lost Girl
to Tiger Lily

At birth, I was instructed to select a prince
and not a career.

I was shown how to look and act like a lady
to appease my prince
instead of being taught how to read or write.

And even after dedicating the first part of my
life to trying to learn how to live for a man
instead of myself, I ran from my life thinking
there must be more to this.

But I only found myself stuck
until a pixie showed me the
path to a star.
And now I am lost, waiting to be
found.

The Will Of A Dying Artist

The Second Lost Boy
about the author

Why have you brought me here, mother?
I weep because I've
lost my wings
in the process of departing from
heaven in your womb.
Now they are removing my
body from your own.
Perhaps I am free but
I am all alone.
I haven't a clue of
what I should do.
I want to leave, mother.
Which way leads back to heaven?
How long will it be before I return?
I am frightened, mother, deathly afraid.
I feel that any of these creatures would
harm me if they could.
I feel that some of them don't want me here
living beside them.
I feel that most of them are indifferent and
couldn't care less either way and are searching
for the way back to heaven as well.
I never asked to be here so why, then, am I
trapped?

"Hush, now, my dear child. Everyone asks your
same

The Will Of A Dying Artist

question and everyone thinks they know the answer.
Perhaps it shall be discovered to you if you continue
to live a little while longer."

The Will Of A Dying Artist

The Third Lost Boy
to John Napoleon Darling

Selfishly, he sought all he wasn't given at birth.
Upon discovering that the Earth offered
none of what he truly desired,
he wandered into one of the most magical places
on the planet: the library.
And from a dusty shelf he found himself printed
on crispy,
creamy sheets of paper all of what he truly desired
and more.
It was them and there alone,
breathing in an endless supply of pages
that for a temporary amount of time he
could feel found.

The Will Of A Dying Artist

Harness These Words Close When Nothing Else Is
Hey there, it's okay. I get it. Just hang on a little bit longer.

You're not alone, good children,
For I know how you feel.
Yes, it pains me to this day
and it's most difficult to conceal.
You dream the best
and hope the rest
and so why does it always seem that it's the worst
that is what's real?

Why does your heart skip a beat, pounding against
your chest with anxiety?
Why do you feel so trapped in this life, unable to
break free?
Why does your existence lack a will and your smile
lack glee?
Suzy breaks the glass and dashes
tears drip from your delicate lashes
as you think *"Oh dear, that must've been me."*

You wonder why no one else understands that
death to you equals peace.
And their judgmental reactions make you want
your own existence to cease.
You're tugging at the pant leg of hope,
You're wrinkling the crease.
You're flying but you want to return to land soon
before you fall.

The Will Of A Dying Artist

And if you survive you shan't enjoy a thing but
continue to crawl.

Close up the curtains, mama.
Daylight will blind me.
In bed I wish to stay.
Maybe if I remain here long enough my frozen body will
decay
like my soul
and yes I am whole
but what is it that fills me up
but the emptiness I feel?
I'd rather be empty and sick
than busy falling for the trick
of someone who calls a child a con.

Remember, dear, never blame yourself for how you
can't help but feel.
May I remind you that to their accusations you
never have to kneel?
Never listen to those who haven't jogged a mile
within your broken in shoes.
Allow yourself to feel everything.
Allow yourself to snooze.
You see a dim light, have you any hope at all? The
old man is still singing the blues.
The game is not over and you will not lose.
Time will heal all.
Forgive and let go.
You'll never forget but your strength will always
show.

The Will Of A Dying Artist

Tough it out in time out and in time you will only glow.
You can only be raised from the deep and the low.
Don't run from your life for there's nowhere else to go.
Take it from me, this I know.

The Will Of A Dying Artist

Deforestated

An Ode To War

I hid 'neath a leaf
and panted with grief
as the men came marching by.

To watch my home fall
was most gruesome of all.
I hadn't the chance to wish
my neighbors goodbye.

Only I knew
but instead of fleeing
to the rescue
I shook and waited with fear.

My home is now in shambles
yet the men's mouths are filled with
rambles
of returning to their wives at home.
Their selfish feet stomp and roam.

Now you must see

The Will Of A Dying Artist

why so worried I be.

I am still looking for my family.

I last saw them in our tree

but now my dresser

will be smashed into paper for the men

to use and throw away.

To no one else this I can say
but
I hide in the dark day after day
out of fear that the men will return.
My weak body starves til no fat
hangs from my bones.
Because of them,
my soul will be deteriorated,
my being will be stripped
of the will to live,
all I've ever known will be
bashed.
They'll rejoice as they watch
my tortured body burn.

Their political cause and pure evil,
both of which are difficult to discern,
puzzle my troubled mind.
To this, I am blind.
Over my shivering body I fix the dry fern
and wonder
what it is they've been taught, that they learn
to bring them to do such evil, such sin.

The Will Of A Dying Artist

My hips are small and my hair is thin
and I really do hope there's a war that we'll win
because I don't know how much more of this I can
take.
If I'm stretched any wider I'm bound to break.

The Will Of A Dying Artist

Hope Is Not A Verb,
But A Lifestyle

Someday
I shall find myself
content
and
infatuated
with life
and a soul
across the sea.

Someday
I shall find myself
older
holding
in these same
trembling hands
a handful
of accomplished dreams
feeling whole
and acting as me.

Someday
I shall find myself
riding on a highway
blasting The Beatles
overriding the noises
caused by the wheel's roll.
In perfect bliss I will be.

The Will Of A Dying Artist

I'd like to savour the life
I've been given
before it is gone.
I'd like to explore the world
I've been born into before I leave.
But in this life I feel trapped like a pawn.
And I fear I may not laugh as much and
instead only grieve.

Yet I continue
to eat hope for
breakfast every
morning, convincing
that all will be well
eventually.

Painting

Porcelain

(prejudice & philosophies)

Talking To

Dolls

(politics & philosophies)

The Will Of A Dying Artist

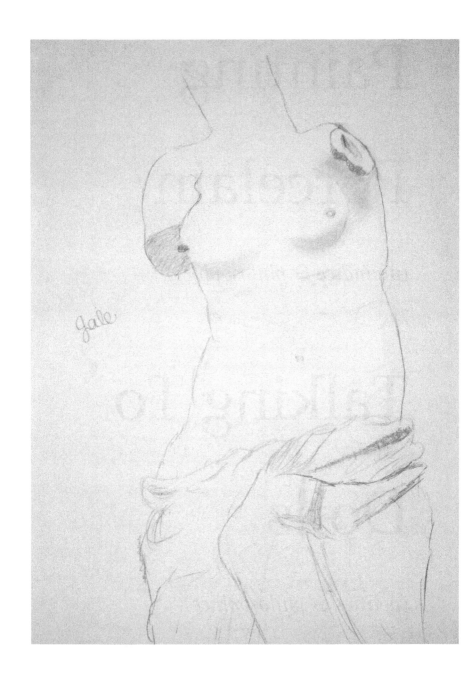

The Will Of A Dying Artist

The Irony Of Timothy Mouse

How funny it be,
what curious things!
The elephants loved the song
until they discovered
it's a mouse that sings.

The Will Of A Dying Artist

Thirst

Crying is another form
of bleeding.
Writing is another form
of crying.
Words, like tears,
are wet.
Be wary,
with each page flip.
You're liable to slip.

Every writer
cries into a bowl
and makes copies
of these bowls
to ship
off to souls
who dip
their hands in this bowl
and drink the tears of a
stranger and recognize the
taste as their own.

The Will Of A Dying Artist

The Very Dark Door of 1964 & After The Fact &
Before

"Pixies are lice!" claim the little mice.

"There's a pixie in my house!"
cried Winfred the mouse
and darting out of the room
came his spouse
running about in a whirl
followed by their little girl
whose tail was in a swirl
whose fur was in a curl
when a tricksy pixie she there saw.
She ate all the eggs raw
and the seeds in the cupboard she'd knaw
and just because she was a pixie she gave herself
the right
and told us we were too below her to fight.
She took all the cheese,
though we begged on our knees.
She told us she needed it for her trip overseas.
"Every pixie's an imp!" declared Winfred the mouse.
"And anyone who can't see this is nothing but a simp"
And on his way to work his head was hung way
down
so a caring pixie grinned at him but he returned to
her a frown.
"I hate those damn pixies. I really hate 'em all.
No pixie is a friend of my daughter's. And if any of them
she tries to call

I'll cut off the phone line and take away her doll."

"I have every right to be bitter and hate. Take a look at the world, look at its state. For me to be like he or she is only my fate." claimed the little pixies.

I hadn't a friend but Lily
with her I could be quite silly.
But I was a pixie and she was a mouse
and her father could be quite a grouse.
Lily, I could no longer call
we couldn't play at all.
I saw her at the store
but me she chose to ignore.
And I silently sobbed thinking
"What on Earth is all of this for?"
"Why does this happen to me?
My only friend is Lily
and she I can never see.
How can this be?"
And her father's illness can spread like a disease.
Around him I began to sneeze.
And one day, I avoided the mice
and only sought a friend in a pixie.
But take it from me.
This is no way to be.
You're blinding yourself.
You can no longer see.

The Will Of A Dying Artist

Take them all off and let your eyes roam free.
They shall thank thee.

The Will Of A Dying Artist

Stripes & Spots

"That is not a human, but a thing!" said Peter
Whose father told him the very same thing.
And naturally Peter was not wrong.
Because the *thing* he mocked looked different from
him.
And because of this it was different.
And because of this it did not deserve to be given
chances.
Because it looked different, and therefore, it lacked
potential.
And Peter's father's father warned his son well.
For this thing was dangerous.
And it was dangerous because he said so.
And as his son, he should listen to him.
And his father before him told him the same.
And his father before him mocked the thing with
the spots on its skin.
Because stripes were much more pleasant to the
eye than spots.
But his father before him had spots as well, in
places no one could see.
And that father before him was covered in spots.
And to his son with stripes, this father said "You
are not a human, but a thing!"
And naturally he was not wrong.
Because the *thing* he mocked looked different from
him.
And because of this it was different.

The Will Of A Dying Artist

And because of it did not deserve to be given
chances.
Because it looked different, and therefore, it lacked
potential.

The Will Of A Dying Artist

Listen Children,
Wise Words From The King's Tongue!

I see you in this way
because you look like this.
You are an animal
you spit and you hiss.
And all of this makes sense
I mean what else could you be?
I mean, after all, you're different from me
as far as I can see.
I refuse you a chance
because although you're a human being
my eyesight is great for I do a lot of seeing
And you're only 1/5 of the human that I am.
Biology proves it, I tell you no lie ma'am.
At birth I shall strip you of all of your rights.
Those babies shall cry, they're allowed zero bites.
Stealing from others the desire to live
shows all the love I have freely to give.
I want you to know that it's you that I judge
because for someone that looks like you I'm
holding a grudge
and the fact that I've even considered that persons
looks
demonstrates my intellect for I go by the books.

The Will Of A Dying Artist

Subtitles

I tied loose bows 'neath
my neck as a headscarf
sat atop my head.

The fridge was much
shorter and much rounder.

Slang has always been silly
and I spoke it fluently like a
language of its own.

Cat-eye frames slipped from
the bridge of my nose.

Rules here, rules there. Rule everywhere.

Some ethics right and fair. Some that brought a
man to change his hair.

Beliefs divided into two.

Country divided into two.

Each person divided into two.

I am one.

American.

The Will Of A Dying Artist

Anthropocentric

We, the people,
enjoy forming the
meanings of words
and explaining why all
is this way and not any
other way.
We are walking, talking
dictionaries of free will.

The Will Of A Dying Artist

Politricks

They were both searching for answers
and discovered half of the truth
staring at opposite ends of the turtle.

They both came to different conclusions
on if the turtle was moving slow at all
and if so how and if so for what reason.

Instead of fixing the turtles broken leg,
however, their ceaseless bickering scared
the poor thing away and the turtle could no
longer move anywhere being blocked by both
groups.

The group behind the creature denied
that the turtle was injured at all and failed to
mention this. The group in front of the turtle
explained the
reason behind the turtles injury in the first place
that had
caused them to fail to pursue any course of action
necessary.

And so the turtle eventually died, abandoned by
both groups and injured severely. Both groups
blamed the other for the turtle's tragic death.
After this turtle's life ended they both went on to
find new turtles, forgetting about the old one and

The Will Of A Dying Artist

gathered together large boulders and tiny stones to begin to build on mountains of excuses as to why all of these turtles kept dying.

Realpolitik

Humans
are funny beings.

They drink liquid
they're only sure is
water because they've
been told such.

They, then,
spit out the juice,
still believing that it's water
and convincing others of
the same.

The Will Of A Dying Artist

Causeries & Clishmacalvers

Reality is not alluded for the sake of it already lacking the meaning of the word real. Reality is alluded to entertain us human beings and make all seem more worth living for than it actually is. Reality is alluded to convince people that our lives are far more interesting and purposeful than that of any other species.

Those who seek truth do so because they truly long for fulfilment. This truth seeking is a concept brewing in the minds of all who aren't satisfied and long for more when there is no more. These are manifested illusions that all believe yet none strive to fix simply because they deem the world superior to them when they, in fact, are the world themself.

So who's afraid of Virginia Woolfe? We all are. And what is to be done? I suppose this is more of a matter of what can be done. Perhaps all seems fake not because it really is fake or was intended as such but because we, the people, haven't a clue what to do or how to behave aside from breathing.

Be wary of disregarding love when love is one of the few concepts that seems real the most. If love seems fake, this is because it is the human beings that are making love out to be such when, speaking of love in terms of a force, this force does not have to be acted upon in vain. If one is to love yet confuse love with foreign principles, diluting it completely, then one is not loving at all but mistaking love with what is not real. If one is giving and receiving love then it is love they shall feel.

The Will Of A Dying Artist

Feral Semantics
— raw, untamed meaning

The next man
contains just as
much complexity
as I.
We just choose to
display our webs
customly.

Why refer to life as
a person when it's the
situation of your society
that you're truly referring
to?
A life is a concept that
describes the breath
occupying the lungs
and the rhythm of the
heart and the blood of
the veins.
A society is a system that
describes the expectations
of a peoples and their
contributions to mankind.

I am a human being born
into a society.
I do not live for or because
of this society.

The Will Of A Dying Artist

I do not live just to live.
I do not live because I am
expected to live.
I live for reasons
I'm living to discover
yet have already found
and am still hanging on
for.

The Wilde Effect

"Art is our spirited protest; our gallant attempt to teach nature her proper place." — Oscar Wilde, 1891 (The Decay Of Lying - An Observation)

Kiss my wooden cheek.
Perhaps I do not speak
but it is joy to you I bring.
I cannot let my opinions sing.

This is why we, dolls, were
first imagined in the form
of women and children.

Drop me and I shall break.
Leave me and I shall wait for you.
I shan't move an inch.
And if ever you tire of me, you
may give me away at your pleasing.
After all, I am yours.

This is why we, dolls, were
first imagined in the form of
women and children.

The Will Of A Dying Artist

The Newton Effect

"   Every object in a state of uniform motion tends
to remain in that state of motion unless an external
force is applied to it.   "   — Isaac Newton

All that happens,
has happened,
and ever will happen
be it so because
some force has acted upon
a situation to make it as it is.

All that is,
has been,
and ever will be,
are
because everything
around this object
contributed something
to its creation.

Perhaps
everything does
happen for a reason.
But that reason is formed
by something acting upon this
portion of everything

The Will Of A Dying Artist

to make it how it is.

Do not say
*if it is meant to be
it will be*
because
humans are
beings of free will and
not entirely instinct
and therefore, we are
provided the power
to change what will be
before it even is.
If we do not act
upon anything
then we are lazy
and fooling ourselves
with excuses.

The Will Of A Dying Artist

1¢ Per True Word

If words are not true
then words are not new.

Human being
mean what you say
when you speak it.
Otherwise don't bother
to leak it.

Because faux
words make everything
around us seem faux
and when reality begins
to feel like an illusion,
our minds fill with confusion.
And we resort to art because
escapism feels most real
and this is why
life imitates
art just as
art imitates life.

The Will Of A Dying Artist

An Affair With What Could Be

Possibility
is the seemingly alluring thief that causes my
annually starved
heart to spread her lips
and my naive lips to drool out waterfalls
because the whole
idea of possibility
are weights for the last, lazy ounces of hope left
lying around within me.
As a dreamer, I live because
my very will to live is built upon the exact fantasies
I am never certain
will occur.
But taking risks is only in my nature.
This is the very
reason I have unpeeled myself
exposing the raw potato I am
for who I am,
only to be mashed.
Yet, still,
possibility is like a perfectly proportioned lover for
my heart to lust over.
Whenever possibility enters my life,
he is my hearts newly wed lover on his honeymoon
with that young, gullible organ.
My heart is never aware that she is being stripped
into vulnerability for disappointment.
But my heart has been starved for so long
that the poor thing cannot be blamed

The Will Of A Dying Artist

for willing to take the risk/
As a result of this, she lies
to me to convince me that all will be fine
because she is selfish
and doesn't
care that my mind punishes me
for every emotion she makes me feel
bringing me one step closer to
possibly
dying.
But then again,
this
possibility
comforts me
and
puts me at ease
in the midst of an
overbearance of stress
because I can always convince myself
that if all goes
wrong
there is a way out
even when there isn't.
But where would I be
if I weren't hanging on
to the omnipresent lover
that leaves and returns as he pleases?
Possibility.

Trails

Left

Behind

(what people can do)

The Will Of A Dying Artist

The Will Of A Dying Artist

Quilts

I sewed our memories into my life
but you loosened the stitch we tied.
I wrapped my shameful, naked body in the
colorful patches of our creation last night because it
was rainy and cold
and I wanted to feel warm and dry but it was
difficult to feel that way without you.
When I reached out to you this morning, you took
your scissors and cut me off.
Because you're sewing warmer, thicker, more
colorful quilts with people I'll never be.
And now my quilt is too small and thin to warm
my fragile bones.
And even if I tried to sew stitches on my own
my tears would make my fingertips slippery
and I wouldn't be able to slip the string
through the needle.
Besides, you've
always been
better at
that
than
me.

The Will Of A Dying Artist

Playing Pretend

The first time I was kissed by a boy
he not only devoured my lips
but my entire face.
My chin was
drenched in
saliva.
I had
to wipe
my face
several times
before he went in again.
And he continued to kiss me
as if his face were attached to my own
by some unbreakable translucent string.

I could scarcely breathe then.
My youthful body no longer
felt like my own but his,
for my lips were his.
They belonged to

The Will Of A Dying Artist

                                                him.
                                                 To
                                                him
                                          I belonged.
                                        I allowed him
                                      to decide just the
                                    way everything would
                                   be. If he told me to move
                                to the closet, I would follow.
                              If he told me to slip beneath the
                    sheets, I would follow him under the covers.

I can recall him making himself
right at home over my pounding
chest. His mouth should've been
dry by the time our multiple
make-out sessions had
come to a close because
every drop of spittle
from that boys
tongue was
transmitted
onto my own.
I had failed to
label this strange
but pleasurable sensation
at that age for all I knew was
that for some unexplainable reason
I liked the feeling of the mouth of an
older boy glued to mine and did not want this

unfamiliar sensation to be put to an end anytime
soon.

At that age, the only word I could concoct
to describe the lust I felt was nervousness because
of the
unapologetic way my heart pounded as if it were
poking at
my chest with knives in a daring attempt to slice it
open and escape.
It was *nervousness* I felt that caused my pits and my
neck and every inch
of me with the ability to move to sweat with what
Eddie Cooley described
as fever. My temperature had risen and my limbs
had gone numb for
they refused to move less he moved them for me.
And the irony of
the situation was that neither of us had felt any
particular way
about the other. He kissed me because his
premature heart
was a scientist coaxing him into testing out its
hypothesis. I was but a lab monkey feeding
the endless imagination of this human
who had, possibly, had his every
nerve stimulated from one
touch and needed to see
what a kiss had the
capabilities of

doing.

The Will Of A Dying Artist

The Fairy Of Her Fairytale

Perhaps
the very reason
I always confuse
fantasy with reality
is because the very first
time I was *kissed*
was in the midst
of child's play.

The boy
who *kissed* me
for the very first
time can never recall
what took place that day.
And this is by no fault of his own.

I was but a babe
and his premature tongue
was sweating with saliva and
a lust he couldn't quite understand himself.
I guess it was his animal instincts that forced it out
of him.
I don't think it was me he desired at all.
For he was just a male dying to
experiment this natural
sensation onto a female
and I suppose I was
convenient enough
at the time.

The Will Of A Dying Artist

All was done in the dark
and I hadn't a clue of what
it was that was taking place
even while it was happening.
All I knew was that this human
being was pressing his lips against
my own and shoving his tongue down
my throat and for some oddly human
reason this act called a kiss didn't feel bad
but good and so I allowed it to continue.
Thankfully he wore pants to cover what didn't
need to be exposed but he wore no shirt to cover
his heaving, bare chest.

The
next
time
I am
kissed
I'd like the
reason to be
because the
individual
signing his name
in my mind with
his tongue contains
a heart pounding with
more than lust and curiosity
and preteen hormones for a
little girl years younger than him.

The Will Of A Dying Artist

Dear, God, I hope that the next time
I am kissed it is because the heart of a
King is overflowing with an invincible
love to the point it causes his healthy
heart to ache so his body must
disregard his conscience and
give a single kiss to the
Queen in
order to
seal a
royal
alliance
of two
pure
hearts.

The Will Of A Dying Artist

The Unwanted Toys Jam

Every woman's a heartless snake.
It's me they're determined to break.
She questioned my masculinity.
She called me a *she* instead of a *he*.
She fought me to the death.
We exchanged harsh words and foul breath.
She demeaned me for my height
and called me weak and lacking might.
She forced my fat to burn so that
muscles would replace the meat.
She told me to leave if I couldn't take the heat.
She wanted my sunflower to grow
because there were seeds she wanted to sow.
She wanted a Gaston
with a chiseled chin
and the build of a faun.
She wanted slicked back hair
but she did not seem to care
that her every word I would hear
and for her I was always there
and I constantly made the effort to be near.
Perhaps I'm not as
tough
or strong
or simple
as he.
But unlike the man to
sweep you off your feet
I shall care indefinitely.

The Will Of A Dying Artist

He's a brute
but to you I am a flea.
Chasing what I can never touch
shall always be me.

The Will Of A Dying Artist

The Unwanted Dolls Fix

Unrequited beau,
why do you indulge in such
pleasure
in torturing me so?
Fling my all at you
I do
but you seem to be occupied
with that of who?
Alas!
Tis the lass
that pays you no mind.
I accept your every flaw
and she's treating you unkind.
How on Earth do I reach you men?
This I fail to understand.
Perhaps if I avoid you like she
on Plymouth Rock I shall land.
It seems you crave what you cease to obtain
and when it is this you finally gain
it is a bore.
My letters to you, you tore.
I broach out my philosophies
while you snore.
Now you have left me
as a thumb that is sore
and I have decided lock my door
because of this game that I fancy no more.

How Wise,
Ordinary
And
Practical
People
Fall
Into
Love

They don't
because though
such qualities in the
personalities of men
exist, none override the
predominant nature of a
man unveiled.
Therefore,
wise,
ordinary
and
practical
people
are more
than simply
incapable of
falling in love.
All that sounds
practical
and
wise

The Will Of A Dying Artist

and
ordinary
to the ears
of these
strange,
rare
beings
is none
other but
the ability
to reproduce.

How
Girls
Fall
In
Love

When he winked at me
the sun's beams opened
my petals and I blushed.
The sensation of my
petals being exposed
to the light set my
heart aflutter.
"He is the one
for me." said
I. *"Because he*
is the cause
of my blooming."
But his true intentions
became clouded. Some
days he would water me
with affection and others
he neglected me entirely
preferring to pay
more attention and care
to the other flowers in the
garden. I almost died without
a proper supply of water.
The rain came by one night
so that the sound of my

The Will Of A Dying Artist

weeping wouldn't be heard.
The rain saw how
thirsty I was, how I
was dying for a drink
and provided me with
fresh water. The rain opened
my eyes and soothed my roots.
This is none other but a common
way that girls stretch into women.
It was at the point and a few others
succeeding it that I began to fall in love as a
woman.

How
Women
Fall
In
Love
an explanation for
the broken male heart

One must be able
to cunningly slice open
the beating heart of a woman
without her realization or consent
and place within it images of thyself
to be transported to the mind, feelings
of intoxication without pouring alcohol into
her throbbing chest and faint signs of assurety
that she will be cared for in your presence.
One mustn't use a double-edged sword to
tear at her delicate chest for she is sure
to be aware of all that is happening and
flee from your side. One mustn't place
images of thyself acting out immorally
with the likes of other women within
her heart to be transported to the
mind. One mustn't get her drunk
on you and leave her waking
alone covered in booze and
shame and a hangover
enough to make her
avoid you for as
long as she

The Will Of A Dying Artist

breathes.
Nothing
you say
to her
at this
point
will
she
be
quick
to believe.

How Writers Fall In Love
about the author

Stage I
Dance

A series of infatuation-stuffed sighs can be overheard from the flushed lily whose petals are wilting from the depth of the rough poetry slipping from a nearby throat. The young lily remains speechless, her stem quivering in the soil surrounding her uncontrollably at the very sound of a flavorful accent sprinkled over a silky voice to coat it, filling her with a half-empty sensation of invigoration. The few petals remaining atop her swayed with the breezes to the music of the words she witnessed from a figure she could hear as clear as day yet ceased to see. She envisioned a twisting beacon of raw romance and weeped as dozens of tingles teased pricked her drunken heart simultaneously. My petals fall for voices comparably to how lilies dance to spoken word traveling through the wind.

Stage II
Flight

The hopeful bluejay passed a feather plucked from her arm onto the robin that had set her eyes aflame with every flap and flick of the tongue. The robin

The Will Of A Dying Artist

had eyed her in a way she longed to be looked upon; with a keen, undying intrigue. An accidental nudge on her shoulder had formed a rope that refused to be loosened. For she was just as good as attached to the robin like a limb on his body, flying behind him wherever he went. She was driven by his charisma, addicted to the druggy way it caused her to feel. He willingly took the feather from her with a smile that was sharp and reflected subtlety. My feathers fall for attitudes comparably to how one bird flies behind another.

Stage III
Transformation

The caterpillar wrapped itself in a snug cocoon and waited with humble patience as the potential-filled fetus slowly transformed into a creature capable of soaring. With every genuine moment shared, I become more of a creature of beauty than intended. With enough time I could lift myself off my toes and float atop the air. I, eventually, grow wings when treated sincerely romantically comparably to the death of a caterpillar developing into the birth of the butterfly. At this point, I can fly high enough to breathe in mirage and truth, to be inspired to make art. I shall convert love into art for as long as I breathe.

Stage IV
Eruption

The Will Of A Dying Artist

In the stage of swooning, a volcano is hit releasing
concern and care from the cracks entering my mind
through my nose. I begin to tremble comparably to
how a volcano erupts when fiery magma of love
and emotion are too much to bare and explode
within the heart. By the time I find myself shaking,
I am usually forgotten, not being aware of all the
truth that was revealed from the explosion. Not
being aware that wherever truth is revealed,
destruction follows since the hearts of men are only
amused by what they are unable to touch.

The Will Of A Dying Artist

How
Poets
Fall
In
Love

Pour the liquor
of your brain onto my
tongue so that I can become
drunk on your every thought.
Unpeel yourself for me so we
can converse as if we haven't a
notion of what it means to be
grown and practical.
Enlighten me.
Hark as I
sing opera
in a fashion
formed to woo
you and to disguise
all I am truly saying
with icing and sugar
so that the innocent
truth of all that I am
won't be used against
me in the near future.
For every bat of the eye,
lick of the lips and sigh
of the mouth a stanza
shall be formed in your

The Will Of A Dying Artist

honor. I shall make the
beat of your heart rhyme
and the stomp of your foot
feel as if me being approached
by you is identical to being taken
by the hand and lifted from my feet.

The Will Of A Dying Artist

How I Fall In Love

Mystery turns me on.

Don't store away the trash
that will spew from your
mouth at 3 in the morning.
You will know that
I
          have
already
                    fallen
       for
             you
when I begin to study these pieces of
trash, adding on to your madness
(simply for the sake of it being *your*
madness and yours alone)
with my own propositions like a
drunkard.

I'd like you to draw a portrait of me
so that I can be certain you don't see
me in a way that does no justice
to the work of art I truly am.

I need to be certain you think I am
greater than I truly am before
diving into the bottomless pool that
conveniently
managed to make its way near me

The Will Of A Dying Artist

around the exact time of your presence
and allowing
myself to drown in your every word.

I am poetry.
Record me
even if only to be viewed
by my eyes alone
so that if anything ever
should happen to me
you will have my raw, unclothed
soul to look back upon as a
shameless reminder and a
hand-drawn
portrait of my flesh and bones
before they withered away.

Don't mistake me for someone
who is selfish when playing this game.
True, be not alluded when I warn you that
you shall be craved and thought of constantly
and endlessly. For you will be the very reason
that sore legs skip out of bed in the mornings and
dark faces flush a complete rosy red.
But I have drawn many more portraits of you and
and have written an incomparable amount of
poetry because of you than you will ever be aware
of.

Be mysterious

The Will Of A Dying Artist

so that my heart may race
and the corners of my mouth may drool
with thirst
and my pencil will possess a mind of its own
when I pick it up and set it to paper.
Allow me to solve your mystery and I will be
forever attached to you.
Even when you lay awake and ceilings are
about to crumble from being stared at by you
for too long, you will be thought of.
Disregard my eyes
and I shall soon
busy myself with
matters I should've been
focusing on to begin with.
Stare into my soul
with eyes that never change;
eyes that are, in itself, your soul
and you can rest easy with the assurance
that I am being tortured every moment I must
be forced to imagine your stare instead of reliving
this invigorating sensation if only once more.

Randevu

Time is an illusion
manipulating my life.
Why do I wait as floods
of tears drip from these
agitated, sizzling balls
of vision glued to my
face
to be left abandoned
by that of whom
claims to care
but apparently not enough
for such things not to be of the matter?

Why did I expect the good to come
when
usually from my life it likes to run?

My reality feels unbearable, like a
colossal waste of time.
I want to trap myself in movies, books and rhyme.

Never again, I say, shall I try such a thing.
Nothing but sorrow and disappointment does it
bring.

The Will Of A Dying Artist

Two Drifters
— *analogy from "Moon River" by Johnny Mercer*

I long to feel wanted
as if with every word
I speak I'm filling your
life to the brim with
the very essence of
adventure instead of
boring you half to death
with words you'll forever
fail to recall.

If only it was I receiving
the call instead of having
to hook my excuses onto
the end of the fishing rod,
tossing it into the stream
where you live, hoping you'd
catch on. You'll fancy me odd
upon discovering that you were
not reeled in to be cooked and
delivered into my greedy belly
but only to capture your
attention so we could swim
alongside one another.

You speak of all your happenings
as if they are casual, trivial,
daily activities. And with this I begin
to feel shame for the fact that when

The Will Of A Dying Artist

you answered my call you were
already preparing yourself for a
round of show-and-tell yet my pockets
were empty.

Shock was immediately fired throughout
my nerves alerting me so suddenly when
you so casually confessed that you fancied
me strong as if I hadn't a care in the world
when just a little while before the call I was
silently contemplating ending the game,
convinced I was the weakest human being
on the planet for trying to escape.
I cared about everything and felt it all much
too strong and perhaps it was this that was
killing me.

I could not feel numbness any longer.
I could only feel all that barrelled my way
for my mood was much more sensitive
and flexible and undetermined than the untamed
sea.

You speak of all you've been doing and your
experiences with people you've met and I
can't help but notice that I am missing from this
picture.
I have tried to allow you to live without me
but I suppose this has been difficult because
I am still growing, you see.
I am still learning how to allow days and nights

to speed past me without feeling the need to
contact another.
Do I lie to myself about all that is, concocting the
silliest of notions that practical people could easily
see through?

Perhaps I am mad for acting as if fantasy is real.
Only dreamers understand how it feels to be
awoken
from a dream so suddenly.
To realize that the characters in the movie you're
watching
are only figments of someone's imagination and
not
heros you can meet and befriend.
To set aside a book because of the pain this tiny
masterpiece causes you to remember feeling just as
the character is, in your own life
once you realize that your eyes are only scanning
pages and your feet aren't actually walking
whenever
the character you believed you were takes a step.

The Will Of A Dying Artist

Paradox Of The Overly Passionate

I shamed myself for
enjoying their kisses
because they were just as I.
Therefore I must've been immoral
and the way I felt couldn't
have been natural.

I worked myself up to the point
of regurgitation out of acknowledgment
of the shameful sin that embodied my
every thought and my own pitiful
insecurity.
Confession freed me of suffocation
for the time being.
No longer do I feel as I did.
No longer do I see as I did.

To my relief,
I feel matured
in this area.
With each and every
passing, wasted day.
I feel like I'm stretching
into a woman.

The Will Of A Dying Artist

Solo System

Stretched.
I am being stretched out
all the way without my consent.

The connections with people I
once cherished are withering
away from my life; disintegrating
into ashes.

In place of this, I have been given
time to work on my relationship
with myself.

I can no longer continue to take
what is given to me from the outside
world, damaging the sacred sections
of my heart in the process.

I must allow myself to feel so that my
already bursting heart may be expanded
upon.

I am a never ending construction site.

I mustn't continue to blame myself
for not understanding the equation the first
few times it's been explained to me.
I must live this equation to understand it.
I do not need to memorize the formulas.

The Will Of A Dying Artist

All that is necessary is practice which will
always be given to me, even at times I fancy
it the most unnecessary of tasks.

I must be the person to acknowledge and
accept the fact that I do try every single day.
I must be the person to lift my spirits in the midst
of my sorrow.

The Will Of A Dying Artist

Drive-in

One of my greatest fears is of returning to the
places that I've already been.
Not only will I be forced to remember all as clearly
as a movie playing out in front of me on the big
screen of a drive-in but I will be forced to form new
memories in place of the old, permanently
demolishing what once was.

Zeit | |<u>geist</u>

(how remembering feels)

The Will Of A Dying Artist

Intrinsic

I was there, I was there.
When the jukebox filled the air.
I was tapping the checkered floors
with my bobbysocks stuffed in my
brown and white
saddler shoes.

There was I, there was I.
Thick hair greased up high.
A cherry popsicle dripping from my chin.
Enlarged pupils raised to the
sky.

There I was, there I was.
From my plaid skirt, picking fuzz.
Skipping to hopscotch on the cement.
Toss a stone, feel mighty free.
Where it lands is where it's meant.
Every time I visit is where I'm, then, supposed to
be.

The Will Of A Dying Artist

Beehives & Beetles

Do you believe it possible to feel another time and
travel there?
What I'm implying is this nostalgia— it has always
been so near.
I am but a girl of many dreams, you see.
When I dance, it's with the fairies...
When I read, I'm above the clouds...
And 10 feet tinier with squirrels I sip tea.

I can't shake the feeling that I've been here before.
I care not if I'm rich or poor
but if when I leave this world once more,
content is my restless soul.

Silly am I
to gape and sigh
at postcards that have been used and thrown away.
That foreign time, that foreign day
feels like home.
And why, then, do I roam?

Being here feels surreal.

The Will Of A Dying Artist

The years that I've lived I refuse to conceal.
I welcome this life with an open mind.
It has done me in bitter, it has done me in kind.

For this phenomenon, the explanation
baffles the mind of its very own creation.
I cannot explain what I cannot not recall.
I feel my memories, I feel them all.
In this life, I do not live but dream.
In this life, I breathe instead of scheme.

Mirrors only reveal to me a vessel.
It is with my mind I constantly wrestle.
History alone is visible in the places to which I go.
All has been done, I've seen this show.
In this world I wander. In this time I am stuck.
By the end of this life, I shall rest with any luck.

What has happened before won't let me be.
I don't have a way of making you see
or proving the science of my wandering soul.
I am a spirit beyond your control.

Aging Youthfully

With a stomach protruding,
and crooked teeth opposing,
and cracked lips moist with saliva and blood,
and fingernails short and plain like that of the male,
she twirled a frizzy grey hair 'round her fat,
wrinkly finger.
Heart racing 1,000 miles a minute.
Pits sweating like that of the cowardly lion.
But with the posture of a knight and the smile of a
Queen
she was the intricate essence of the female.
Her eyes hid the fear palpitating within her heart
repeatedly.
She did not fidget like she did as a young girl.
She was well aware of the bags beneath her eyes
and the false teeth glued to her gums and the
wrinkles on the bottom that used to be smooth.
Yet she gracefully carried herself wherever the road
took her.
In adolescence, she fretted and frolocked over what
would become of herself in old age.

The Will Of A Dying Artist

And now that she was there, she unceasingly
longed for all that could've been done in the height
of her youth.
At 67, she was a lonely old woman proudly
ordering a happy meal for nostalgia's sake.
She was watched and mocked as she made her way
to an empty seat near a window.
Removing her four piece chicken nuggets from the
crinkling, paper bag she searched for the toy that
had filled her heart with such joy as a child.
Placing the undersized, breakable paper crown
upon her head, she smiled majestically.
It was then that she was approached by a lonely
little girl with two pigtails in her hair, gazing up at
her with wide eyes and an amused grin.
"Are you a Queen?" asked the child, hesitantly,
fidgeting with her fingers.
"That I am" replied the woman.
"How did you become a Queen?" queried the
curious girl once more.
"Well, child," began the woman in a gentle,
motherly voice, "I was crowned Queen of my own
life at birth. I was raised without knowing my true
royal identity and spent most of my life in vain,

powerding my face with oily substances and filling
my body with fatty sugars. I fell for filthy ogres
disguised as princes instead of handsome princes
disguised as ogres. But now that I feel free, I have
crowned myself Queen once more. And I am
passing my crown unto you. Never lose it."
And with a wink she crowned the child whose
gullible heart beat fast
and watched with a sense of satisfaction as a
confident smile embodied her youthful lips.
The Queen and the princess dined together that
afternoon, disguised as common women in a
modern time.
An unbreakable bond.
An invincible beauty.
Her majesty was no longer a mentality nor was she
a character created for child's play.
She was her majesty when she spoke to the highest
of men without uttering a stutter.
She stared Kings dead in the eye without failing to
reveal all she stood for.

The Will Of A Dying Artist

June 4th, 2017

She must be mad if she thinks she can remember
her thoughts from when she was just a caterpillar
in her mother's womb.

"But oh yes!" she exclaims, "They were the purest
thoughts indeed!"
I had to stop her. "You had no thoughts before you
were conceived."
Foolishly, she persisted, "If humans knew no pain,
nothing but love would fill our voids."

The Will Of A Dying Artist

9th Life Blues

Spend this life, I do
remembering
all of which I fail to recall.

Waste this life, tis true.
This youth means
nothing at all.
I seek all that has been
discovered.
I'm ill though I've just recovered.

Sitting in the heat of day
atop the dewy grass I lay
and to the good lord I say,
*"Carry out your will for my
life today."*

From violence, I wish to flee.
In silence I hope to be.
Perhaps I have no right to cry
when others are struggling to
stay alive and are grateful for
each and every day.
But what else can I say?
Too old and brittle do I feel.
The reel of the years I cease
to conceal.

The Will Of A Dying Artist

The flowing of tears are born of
the sting from the peel
when my skin was pulled in an
attempt to reveal
all that is earnest and real.
Instead of what was expected,
the blood from my veins
was shot upwards,
hitting you in the eye
yet you still failed to see.

If truth is not to believed then
what am I still doing here?
And what is wrong with me?
And sayeth I then, what *should* I be?

The Will Of A Dying Artist

Old Soul Blues

I have grown out of feeling nostalgic for all that has
been.
I, now, regret all that could be but is not.

The Will Of A Dying Artist

Riverbank Blues
— *for banka*

Heat is brutal.

Bees only burn.

It is for the mountains I yearn.

Flat and empty suburbs leave me feeling sore.

I am in constant need of so much more.

Evergreens are damp, dull fiends.

I don't even know what a season means.

All is noisy, all is new.

Take me back to times I once knew.

The sky is either grey or blue.

The stars never come out of hiding.

Even the lizards are chirping and chiding

from humidity hogging fresh air.

Oh, candid country, I wait for you here.

Soon, there shall be here

and here now shan't be near.

The Will Of A Dying Artist

Blanket Fortress
– for Noah

I prayed it to God,
I wished on a star.
And either mustn't have been too far
because out of mother's womb you came:
a baby boy so brazen, so tame.

We stuck you in an empty crib
and gave to you a white and blue bib.

My brother is like no other.
He plays rough but he has a clean heart.

My brother is like no other.
His tongue is plain but his soul is art.

Boil and banter as we do
none of which are ever true.
They've called me a poor sister
but they should shut their trap
because you and I can read each other
quicker than a map.

I hope you grow into a man of your own.
I hope you'll call me on the phone.

I hope with words you'll take good care
even when I am no longer near.

The Will Of A Dying Artist

I hope you'll select a woman that will suit you.
Never let her harm or boot you.

If there's no one else around remember
I wanted you before you were even born.

Because I've always been a lonely child.
To have you, mother's body was torn.

And I'll care for you until time ends.
Because we're not only siblings but
inseparable friends.

The Will Of A Dying Artist

July 4th, 2018

When heads are rested on arms, angels are present.
Love escapes the heart filling the air and humans
are reminded why they've decided to continue
living.
Mommy rested her loving head on my shoulder
and for one still moment in time, home breathed in
my face and kissed my brow.

The Will Of A Dying Artist

Paradox of the Inevitably Old

Why is it that a song from 1931 touches me so
deeply?

Why is it that
my tired eyes cloud with salty tears
and my heart mourns as if upon hearing this very
same tune
native to its time,
 something different was occuring?

My soul is instantaneously enkindled
because I can recognize this tune
but can't seem to pair it with when or how or why.

And I do not *know* this for certain because what
evidence could I possibly present?
But I needn't prove myself to anyone, especially
with a part of me as delicate as my soul and its
whereabouts.
Only within myself can I feel what I do and
through how I feel does assurety follow.

My gut has always forced me to suffer through and
gulp down this pleasant agony in large portions.
But for now I can listen and sway to these tunes
as the same person I was then reborn once more
into this life
into this time
into this body

The Will Of A Dying Artist

with a mind that can and can't remember all at the
same time
and eternally reminisce over times I shan't recall.

The Will Of A Dying Artist

When Rose Wilts,
Who'll Breathe Oxygen Into The Man?
— Ode To Mom

Mother,
my throat is sore.
Pour chamomile tea on my tongue
and soothe the words that fear feeds.
The atmosphere enjoys influencing my mind.
The poison my mind injects into my fragile heart
gets caught in my throat and prickles it like pine
needles.

Mother,
I've caught another fever.
I began to feel ill after I asked
and was promised only for this promise
to be thrown into a pile and forgotten just as before.
Upon this occurrence, chills overtook my tender
skin
and I forced myself to spend too much time
outside, believing
the fresh air was good for me.
But it was raining
and I managed
to convince
myself
it was
not.
Place a
hot rag on my

The Will Of A Dying Artist

forehead and rock
me to sleep in your arms
until my temperature is regulated
and my heart is restored with hope until I
get sick
once
more.

Mother,
I cannot rest.
The spirits lurking
in my dark bedroom
trying to get my attention
are keeping me awake because
they died and they want to remind
the living that their life had purpose too.
And I suppose I'm only afraid of them because
I fear I'm not living my own in the way I should be
and I worry I shall regret all that has been done
when my time arrives.
But for some reason,
when I sleep next to you
as you trace my face, losing sleep
so that I may drift off and you wrap
me in your warm embrace, the spirits
no longer bother me because they see love
and they only prey on the undeniably lonely
and hopeless
and cold
so that
the

The Will Of A Dying Artist

love
they
lack
in death
will be bearable.

Mother,
I scraped my knee
falling from a bicycle
I was forced onto but
never properly prepared for.
I wish I could use my training wheels
but the other kids would only laugh at me.
So I must resort to falling until I finally get the hang
of
playing a sport I was never meant to excel in when
I can
ride my scooter around the block
faster than any of them
can count to ten.

Mother,
I fell from a tree
reaching for the apple
I've planned my whole life
to attain and I almost got it too.
And since a ladder costs money we don't
have, I'm climbing up the old-fashioned way.
And I know the tree is very high and that someone
faster and more skilled than I might reach the apple

The Will Of A Dying Artist

before I do and that it may fall before I get there
and that
it may be harder to pick from the tree than I've
imagined but
I *shall* pick this apple even if I die from falling from
a deadlier height than before, before I get the
chance to taste it.

Mother,
I'll always need you.
I still don't understand
the way the world you brought
me into works and I still don't know
how or why I'm expected to survive it.
But I *am* trying in every way I know how to.
And without you warming my heart when it
freezes,
my heart would crack from being left alone in the
snow.

The Will Of A Dying Artist

From Heaven To Hell And Back

My longings urge me to breathe in the sweet
grasses of paradise.
The scent of fresh sap from the pine trees make
love to my nostrils.
To savour the taste, if only for the most miniscule
of moments,
my dried tongue would be eternally content.
God pasted these two feet onto the bottom of these
two legs so that
I could sink my toes into warm sand and rub my
heels against cool rocks.
Heaven and hell reside on Earth.

How can one stuff their overfilled mouths to the
brim until their shirt buttons
loosen whilst suping and dining in front of a child
intoxicated by starvation in the
process of keeling over?
How can one refuse another their birthright
necessities of life in the midst of sickness
and ailing and disease?
Those blessed with more money than needed were
only provided with such
to put to use for those in need of more money to
survive and thrive.
What brings one man to devote their life to
deriving pleasure from another individual's harm
and destruction?
Heaven and hell reside on Earth.

The Will Of A Dying Artist

The sooner my departure from society arrives,
the sooner I shall be granted the will to live.
Take me to the woods to live as an elf would:
isolated from all in a miniature, quiet cottage.
I seek solace and peace.
Away from the race, involved in focused chore
and balance should I be farthest from sin and
temptation.
I seek an invincible, undeniable nearness to God
that the distraction of money and debt could never
offer.
Heaven and hell reside on Earth.

Why refuse your fellow man the respect they
deserve?
Prejudice is evil's child.
Prejudice is the food for the evil that is injected into
the breast
of mankind, corrupting their beating hearts until
they stop beating.
Raw prejudice in every subtle form is the key to
unlocking the door
to loneliness.
Man's highest peak of loneliness is felt when a
connection to another
is broken off due to the man-made concept of
sunder.
Whatever it is that sets oneself apart from another
dwells in the mind
alone.

The Will Of A Dying Artist

Heaven and hell reside on Earth.

Moonlight engulfs me as I prance to Nat King Cole
and am sprinkled with the tinsel that makes my
fading heart whole.
Twas a Winter's night
when the people of the Earth should feel at home.
Hanging from a branch on a pine is a twinkling
Christmas light.
Bliss thrives in the hearts of children as games are
played on sidewalks
and winks are cast at the still garden gnome.
Heaven and hell reside on Earth.

The Will Of A Dying Artist

Bumblebees Swarm Wherever Pollen Resides

Fairies love to dance with children
in the meadows of in between.
They stay around to play for awhile then they
leave, never to be seen.
I was visited by a lovely two I shall not once in my
life forget.
With flower crowns and lovely gowns we splashed
in puddles letting our feet get wet.
They showed me around their beautiful garden as I
dreamed.
Their smiles made me feel full of life and their eyes
sparkled and gleamed.
They paid me a visit at 5 years old and their spirits
were nothing but pure.
However lonely I may have been the power of a
fairy's a cure
tainted my eyes to embrace a world as captivating
as flowers stale from being freshly pressed.
I do believe they were sent by God to inspire me
and make me feel blessed.
At this age, I can still believe and although at times
I may feel stressed,
the solace felt returns to me once more as I write
out this poem though I hardly recall either face.
Only fragments of expressions, the dimples of their
laughter and bodies that pranced with such grace.
They were like angels and I don't believe they had
an ungodly intention in a single bone.
They were friends to me because they could clearly
see that I was a child left alone.
They revealed to me names I'd be a witch to say
because fairies are funny with these things.

The Will Of A Dying Artist

I feel like I've been to all of Faerie now and none of
my journeys required wings.
I was beginning to believe that all of Faerie was a
trick. That all was rooted in bad.
But I remember the garden and the two sisters I
played with and the feelings of bliss my soul had.
And this must be God's doing, I know that it must
be.
I feel it within my soul!
I'll always be a child.
Reckless and wild.
Candid and peaceful and whole.

Asphodels

(stories untold)

The Will Of A Dying Artist

I bitterly regret Lily's death

Because you feared death

I visited him and picked asphodels for you.

But when I tried to return to you, life no longer

wanted me.

So she carried your asphodels to your doorstep

because asphodels are immortal.

And life loves you.

Because I feared life

I left her too soon.

But I write

because

writing is *words that stay*

as Jen said to Kira in *The Dark Crystal*.

And though I fear both life and death, words are

immortal.

The Will Of A Dying Artist

And words love me.

Because we love each other

we don't fear losing love,

but losing one another.

But life hates me.

And life was jealous of our love.

So when I abandoned life, she took you for herself.

And love loves me,

so she'll never let go.

The Will Of A Dying Artist

The Flowerboy

She asked me for roses,
but I gave her my heart instead.
She seized them from my benevolent hand and
then returned to bed.
I could not see her then but I could feel my
pounding heart bleeding.
She blew her nose in its tissue and with her fists she
began kneading.
She exited the room then and handed this
unfamiliar object back to me.
She claimed it was my heart but a heart I could not
see.
I tried to hand it back to her to fix
but she refused and continued demanding roses.

I sold my heart for roses I could not afford.
She took them from me willingly.

The following week, she demanded more.
I sold my soul for roses.
She took them from me willingly.

The Will Of A Dying Artist

A month later, she demanded more.
My mind had parted ways with me.
I had nothing left to sell.
I gave her a kiss on her left cheek.
But no roses appeared there either.
And so she turned her head from me
and handed back the roses.

I told her I did not desire *them*, but *her*.
She told me she did not desire *me*, but *more roses*.
And so I sold the rest of myself to death for a box
full of roses.
They arrived at her door this morning.
I wonder if that was enough.

The Will Of A Dying Artist

I befell in love as a pup...

Iris and I
were as cute as pie.
She made me laugh. She made me cry.
She always was the apple of my eye.

Then I met Suzy Sue.
From Iris's side I flew.
To me, Suzy was true.
But she hadn't a clue
of what I would do
When I saw Mary.

Mary was quite a doll.
She was only 5 feet tall.
But she didn't love me at all.
And she ran off with Paul.
For her he would fall.

Mary's sister Marie
was more of a he than a she.
With me she climbed a tree.
She fell and hurt her knee.
And the sight was quite ugly.
And since she was no longer pretty.
Off to Anne I went to see.

Now Anne I did not like.
She only loved her bike.

The Will Of A Dying Artist

Through trails she would hike.

Laura I loved the most
She was loud and loved to bost
But to her I was a ghost

When I asked her why this way she was
she loudly proclaimed it was because
she was a Queen and I was a liar
and of her I would soon tire
and if I were were a job
then me she would hire
just so me she could fire.

And because she wanted me not,
Laura alone I sought.

The Will Of A Dying Artist

An Unrequited Hermit's Mirage

They think me a man insane.
But little do they know
the pleasurable filling of bees
where hate used to grow.

My mother told me to avoid them
with no reason given.
My mother told me to do as I'm told,
so I cut them all off as if they weren't even liven'.

As a lonely bigot I spent my days.
With mankind I had parted my ways.

Painting maidens never to be held
until that pitiful age was dispelled.

I saw her when I turned 31
with olive skin and the eyes of the sun.
My mother had warned me of the green people
how they weren't sunflowers like us and just the
sepal.

But this was a lady and I was a man.
Why not watch her if I can?
Mother was wrong and so was I.
I wasted my life believing the lie.

Day after day, I visited her there.
Month after month and year after year.

The Will Of A Dying Artist

Today, I am 73.
I saw her but she never saw me.
A criminal is what I would be.

Removing her from the museum wall,
I ran and I ran but from my hands she would fall.
From her I could never part.
In chains at the station, I lost my heart
to a stolen work of art.
I am only
a lonely man in pain.
Now they think me a man insane.

The Will Of A Dying Artist

The Will Of A Dying Artist

結束

(the end)

Acknowledgements

First and foremost, I'd like to thank God and this book for helping to keep me alive through some of my darkest moments.

Thank you to mom and everyone who has ever supported me as a writer.

I'd like to recognize Ellé Om for illustrating/designing the cover of *"The Will Of A Dying Artist"*. The cover was brought to life better than how I'd imagined it in my mind and with it I have eternally innamorata. Contact the illustrator at: zelaluyolilelu on www.fiverr.com.

The Will Of A Dying Artist

About The Author

Gale Thyme is an American 16 year old lifelong poet, novelist, short story writer, and housewife of words in every form.

Inspired by personal experience and influenced by her own personal battles with mental health, *The Will Of A Dying Artist* was formed from blood, sweat, tears and roots from the author's personal life and observation of others. Growing up finding solace in poetry and literature, this collection was pieced together with the intentions of soothing the pain of every human being that is touched by these words.

As a fairy in disguise, Gale draws inspiration from the natural world, medieval tales/folklore and every creature on God's green Earth. As an old soul, Gale enjoys collecting antiques, classic/rare records, old books/films and putting together fifties-esque outfits.

Made in the USA
Middletown, DE
30 June 2021